THE WORLD OF THE
MEDIEVAL KNIGHT

THE WORLD OF THE
MEDIEVAL KNIGHT

A VIVID EXPLORATION OF THE ORIGINS, RISE AND FALL OF THE NOBLE ORDER OF
KNIGHTHOOD, ILLUSTRATED WITH OVER 220 FINE-ART PAINTINGS AND PHOTOGRAPHS

CHARLES PHILLIPS
CONSULTANT: DR CRAIG TAYLOR

HERMES
HOUSE

CONTENTS

INTRODUCTION

At the Battle of Crécy in August 1346 Edward Prince of Wales, the recently knighted 15-year-old son of King Edward III of England, covered himself in glory as he helped the English army to a famous victory over a French force three times its size. One among as many as 30,000 casualties in the French army was King John of Bohemia, one of the greatest figures of 14th-century European chivalry, who had insisted on proceeding into the thick of the battle with his men at arms despite the fact that he was almost completely blind. His corpse was found on the battlefield the next day surrounded by the bodies of his men, who had died defending him and had tied the reins of their bridles to each other so that they would not be driven apart in the mêlée of the conflict.

After the battle Prince Edward (later known as the 'Black Prince', probably because he fought in black armour) paid tribute to King John, who had been killed fighting the Prince and his men, by adopting John's personal crest of an ostrich feather and his motto *Ich dien* (a short version of German *Ich diene*, 'I serve'). In adapted form this crest and motto remains that of the Prince of Wales to this day.

Returning to England in October 1347, after besieging and capturing Calais and negotiating a truce, King Edward and the Black Prince celebrated Christmas at Guildford then held a great series of chivalric tournaments in 1348. At one, in Windsor, the king founded the Most Noble Order of the Garter, dedicated to the Virgin Mary and St George and conceived as a 'Round Table' of knights in tribute to the mythical chivalric warriors of King Arthur. The founder members of the Order of the Garter were mostly veterans of Crécy and cherished companions and opponents of King Edward and the Black Prince at chivalric tournaments. One later story explaining the origin of the Order's badge (a garter) and motto was that it arose from an act of gallantry by the king. It is said that he swept up the garter that had fallen to the floor from the leg of his mistress, the Countess of Salisbury, and put it on his own leg with the words *Honi soit qui mal y pense* ('Shame come to him who thinks evil of it').

ROMANCE OF KNIGHTHOOD

This sequence of events, from the Battle of Crécy to the foundation of the Order of the Garter, captures a great deal of the romance of medieval knighthood. It also encompasses many of the most glamorous aspects of its code of chivalry: triumph in battle for a newly made knight – often called 'winning his spurs'; King John's determination to seek glory as a warrior; the devoted service – even unto death – of his men at arms; the Black Prince's generosity in victory; the siege and capture of a foreign city; jousting in tournaments before admiring ladies of the court; the foundation of an order of knights in celebration of the legends of King Arthur and the knights of the Round Table, but also as a mark of religious devotion to the Virgin Mary and St George; and the gallantry of a knight, in this case King Edward, towards his lady. Yet it presents only one face of medieval chivalry, which in the course of about 500 years across many countries had many varied aspects.

CHANGES IN CHIVALRY

In August 1346, when the future Black Prince won a great reputation for chivalry at Crécy, it was just over 247 years since the European knights of the First Crusade

◄ *The Battle of Crécy. According to one account, Prince Edward was forced to his knees in the mêlée and was only saved from capture by Sir Richard Fitzsimon.*

had recaptured Jerusalem from Muslim forces, in July 1099. This earlier event, although it was followed by a terrible slaughter of the defenders of the city, was celebrated by western churchmen as a holy triumph, while the crusaders who succeeded against all odds in that first venture to the Holy Land were hailed over the ensuing decades and centuries as the perfection of knighthood.

In 1346 the knights of the First Crusade certainly remained an inspiration to those fighting at Crécy, but the crusaders' understanding of knighthood could not be said to be the same as that of the Black Prince or Edward III or their followers. For one thing, religious faith was the principal motive for many knights of the First Crusade, who were fighting in an international Christian army to 'free' the Holy Land from Muslim rule, whereas knights at Crécy were fighting in a national army or alliance of armies in the service of a king rather than of Christ. For another the ideas of courtly love, which developed in the 12th century alongside the growth of elaborate 'Arthurian' and other themed tournaments of the kind later held by King Edward III and the Black Prince, would have seemed quite foreign to the knights of the First Crusade.

▲ *By the reign of Edward III of England (left), the cult of St George (right) as patron of knights was well established. George was originally an Eastern Orthodox saint.*

▼ *Edward III made St George the patron of his chivalric brotherhood, the Order of the Garter. This 15th-century illustration shows the Knights of the Garter revering the saint.*

At one time historians tended to treat the medieval institution of knighthood as if it were unchanging from the time of its development under the Normans in England during the second half of the 11th century, throughout the medieval period. However, it is important to emphasize that knighthood and knights' understanding of chivalry changed over the 250 or so years from the late 11th century to the mid-14th century and again over the next 200 to 250 years from the time of King Edward III of England to the last flowerings of chivalry in the later 16th and early 17th century. One key change was that knighthood became more exclusive: at one time a brotherhood of warriors to which the greatest martial figures could be raised, it became associated with inherited rank, and increasingly limited only to the descendants of knights.

WHAT WAS A KNIGHT?

In origin the knight was a mounted warrior. The word for knight in French (*chevalier*), in Spanish (*caballero*) and in German (*ritter*) means in every case 'horseman'. The knight had a relationship of near-religious intensity with his weapons (principally his lance and sword) and with his horse. In chivalric chansons ('songs')

KNIGHTS IN SERVICE

The English word 'knight' is derived from the Anglo-Saxon *cniht*, meaning servant or young man, and service was a key element in the medieval institution of knighthood and the accompanying code of chivalry. Knight service was the name for the land-holding arrangement within the feudal system, under which knights were given the right to hold land as a fiefdom in return for serving as a mounted soldier, usually for 40 days a year. The knight provided the military service to his *suzerain* (superior within the feudal system) or the king, to whom, initially at least, the land ultimately belonged.

As the social and religious institution of knighthood developed, however, knightly service acquired other important aspects: service to Christ by fighting for the Christian faith; service to the weak and vulnerable by enforcing the peace; service

and romances, from which we learn so much of knights' received wisdom about chivalric warfare, King Arthur had his revered sword Excalibur, and Roland (leading knight of the Frankish king Charlemagne) fought with a magnificent weapon named Durandel. The chanson hero Renaud of Montauban had his famous magical horse Bayard, which could grow bigger or smaller to accommodate riders of different sizes, and the Spanish war captain Don Rodrigo Diaz de Vivar ('El Cid') had his extraordinary steed Bavieca, which refused ever to take another rider after Don Rodrigo's death.

However, the knights who rode as 'soldiers of Christ' to the Holy Land on crusade and those who jousted in the lists to win the favour of their lady were more than just mounted warriors. They certainly honoured bravery and courage, and praised prowess in battle (or in the lists at chivalric tournaments). But they also aspired to a range of qualities such as Christian faith, courtesy, generosity, loyalty and moderation that were connected to a world of social and religious obligations rather than to life in the saddle.

▲ *A portrait of chevalier Philip Hinckaert, depicted with St Philip the apostle, and the Virgin Mary and child shows how key a knight's religious devotion was held to be.*

▼ *Loyalty and honour often led to death. Knights drew inspiration from Roland, who fought to the end to prevent his sword Durandel falling into the hands of Saracens.*

to the knight's lady by winning honour either in combat at a tournament or by embarking on a journey of challenges as a 'knight errant'.

QUALITIES OF THE KNIGHT

The medieval knight's devotion to service, and to the ethical and spiritual aspects of the chivalric code, made him different from a mounted soldier of earlier ages. We shall see that the medieval knights had precursors in the aristocratic elite of the *hetairoi* (companions) who rode into battle with spear and sword alongside the 4th-century BC Macedonian king and general Alexander the Great; they had forerunners also in the cavalry of the Parthian and Roman empires, and in the mounted warriors of the great Frankish kings Charles Martel and Charlemagne. But these Macedonian, Roman or Frankish warriors were not knights in the way of

▲ *The Arthurian knight Sir Galahad was more spiritual aspirant than bloodthirsty warrior. In the Grail cycle of legends, Galahad was praised as innocent and pure.*

▼ *The legend of Richard Coeur de Lion made much of his ferocity. Stories were told of the crusader king's fondness not only for killing but also for eating Saracens.*

the mid-14th-century English knight Sir John Chandos, renowned for his diplomacy as well as his martial spirit and hailed in the chronicles of Froissart as 'the most courteous knight alive', or of 15th–16th century French knight Pierre de Terrail, Seigneur de Bayard, who was known for his spotless honour and carefree manner and declared *Le chevalier sans peur et sans reproche* ('The fearless and blameless knight') – or indeed of great knights in the chivalric literature, such as Roland, or figures of the Arthurian tradition such as Lancelot or Percival.

KNIGHTLY INSPIRATION

Literary representations of knightly virtue were essential to the development of the institution of knighthood. Great deeds of knights were presented by poets and chroniclers as an inspiration to further great deeds of chivalry. The Spanish law codes *Las Siete Partidas*, promulgated in

the mid-13th century by Alfonso 'the Wise' of Castile, declared that 'accounts of brave feats of arms should be declaimed before knights while they ate', to promote deeds of chivalry by generating a desire to outdo great deeds of the past.

In chronicles, chivalric biographies, poems or romances, writers amplified the feats of arms performed by historical figures such as the 11th-century French knight Godfrey of Bouillon, a leader of the First Crusade of 1095–99 and the first 'Defender of the Holy Sepulchre', 12th–13th-century Englishman Sir William Marshal, a peerless fighter at tournaments who was dubbed the 'greatest knight who ever lived', King Richard I of England, celebrated as *Coeur de Lion* ('Lionheart') for his endeavours on the Third Crusade of 1189–92 or of great French generals of the Hundred Years War such as Jean le Meingre, known as Boucicaut. Ancient figures from the biblical and classical worlds, warriors such as the Jewish freedom fighter Judas Maccabeus, Hector of Troy or Julius Caesar were reimagined as knights of chivalry and so presented as exemplars for

◄ *Sir Lancelot, seen here capturing the castle Dolorous Garde, had all the qualities of the perfect knight, but his adultery with Guinevere was a grave failing.*

▼ *French knight Bertrand du Guesclin was famous for rising from relatively humble origins to achieve high office.*

medieval warriors. Other principally legendary figures such as Roland, the Germanic warrior Siegfried, the British heroes King Arthur or Guy of Warwick were likewise presented as protagonists in affairs of the heart at court, as heroes in tournaments or on the field of battle, even as 'soldiers of Christ' on crusade. Medieval knights listened – and were inspired.

Literary figures such as the 12th-century French poet and writer of romances Chrétien de Troyes, the author of five Arthurian romances and the writer who introduced Sir Lancelot into the cycle, played a key role in formulating prevailing images of knighthood. The most important patrons for Chrétien de Troyes and other poets of the time were lords such as Henry I, Count of Champagne (husband of Marie de Champagne, and thus son-in-law of Henry II of England's wife Eleanor of Aquitaine) and Philip, Count of Flanders. These powerful figures were not only supporters of the arts, but financers and patrons of the chivalric sport of tourneying.

Chivalric literature and tournaments developed side by side at noble courts, where knights exhausted after a physically demanding day of jousting in the lists would settle down in the evening to listen to tales of chivalry. The audience had a taste for tales of arms in various settings, whether the Arthurian court, the Holy Land towns familiar to Crusaders, the classical world of Alexander the Great or Hector of Troy, or the battles against hordes of Saracens (Muslim warriors) fought by Charlemagne and his knights.

Another notable patron was Arnold, Lord of Ardres in northern France (the area where in 1520 King Henry VIII of England and King Francis I of France met for the diplomatic encounter and glittering celebration of chivalry remembered as 'the Field of the Cloth of Gold'). Arnold was known to employ separate poets with specialities in tales of King Arthur, the crusades, and Charlemagne's knights.

A 'TRUE AND PERFECT KNIGHT'

These literary representations did not elevate feats of arms alone as an example for the listening knights, but also praised many other gentler qualities that were appropriate for a knight. The chivalric biography of Boucicaut, for example, stressed his religious faith, wisdom and generosity alongside celebrations of his boldness in deeds of arms. In the Holy Grail cycle of the Arthurian romances, which were influenced by Cistercian monks and the mysticism of Bernard of Clairvaux, the Grail knight Sir Galahad was praised for his humble, Christ-like qualities of innocence and purity. He was even said to be a descendant of the biblical hero King David.

The 14th-century English poet Geoffrey Chaucer, in the Prologue to *The Canterbury Tales*, drew a portrait of 'a true and perfect gentle knight'. Chaucer served

He jousted three times 'for oure feith' (in support of Christianity) in 'Tramyssene' (Tlemcen, Algeria) and each time killed his opponent. He was a distinguished knight, who remained humble and modest – and had 'no vileynye ne sayde' (never spoken rudely) to anyone.

THE SURVIVAL OF THE KNIGHT

Chaucer's knight was soon to face new and well-nigh insurmountable challenges. Beginning in the 14th century, the increasing use of artillery guns and the rise of professional soldiers changed the face of warfare and made the knight outmoded on the field of battle; these developments were coupled with the effects of long-term social changes that brought an end to the feudal societies in which knights had emerged and prospered. Yet as a symbol, a literary figure, and a heroic ideal the knight endured. Through the continuing popularity of chivalric romances and particularly of the Arthurian tradition, he has survived as an inspirational figure of what humanity can aspire to, an embodiment of the noble virtues of bravery, strength of character and simplicity of spirit.

▲ *In tournaments knights proved their martial skills before appreciative courtiers. They fought first with lances, then swords.*

▼ *Early artillery cannon were difficult to load and inaccurate but still had a devastating effect against armoured knights.*

as a squire (a young man undergoing training for knighthood) for that great royal patron of chivalry, King Edward III of England, and fought in the Hundred Years War in 1359–60 in France, where he was captured close to Rheims and had to be ransomed as a prisoner.

Chaucer emphasized key qualities of the chivalric code in his knight, who from the first day that he rode out as a knight had 'loved chivalrie, trouthe and honour, fredom and curtesie'. He had, the poet wrote, ridden far and wide 'in his lords werre' (in service of his lord), both in Christendom and 'hethynesse' (heathen lands). The description listed a number of theatres of war in which he had distinguished himself, including Prussia and Lithuania (where English and western European knights fought on crusades against indigenous pagan people), in Granada and north Africa and in Turkey.

TIMELINE OF MEDIEVAL CHIVALRY

732AD In the Battle of Poitiers (Tours), western France, a Frankish army commanded by Charles Martel defeats a Muslim force of the Umayyad Caliphate in Spain, ending a series of Muslim raids northwards into France.

768–814 Charlemagne reigns as King of the Franks. He is later celebrated as a great Christian king and exemplar of medieval chivalric values.

778 A Frankish army commanded by Charlemagne is defeated by Muslim or Basque raiders in a skirmish in the Pass of Roncesvalles in the Pyrenees mountains. Charlemagne's knight Roland is killed.

842 'War games' at Strasbourg to celebrate the alliance of Charlemagne's grandsons, Louis the German and Charles the Bald, are a forerunner of the tournament.

911 Viking chief Rollo or Robert is granted land in western France by King Charles II. His descendants, the Normans, establish an early form of knighthood and a feudal society in Normandy.

955 King Otto I of the Germans uses heavy cavalry to defeat the Magyars in the Battle of Augsburg, a victory celebrated by contemporaries as a great triumph for Christian knights.

1066 The Normans invade England and defeat King Harold at the Battle of Hastings. William, Duke of Normandy, becomes King William I of England and imports a feudal society and the Norman form of knighthood.

1095 Pope Urban II calls the knights of Christendom to liberate Jerusalem from Muslims, launching the First Crusade.

1099 The First Crusade ends in triumph as Christian knights capture Jerusalem. In its aftermath the religious brotherhoods of the Knights Templar and the Knights Hospitaller are founded.

1100–35 From the time of Henry I of England (r.1100–35) onwards, kings use paid soldiers as well as knights performing feudal service. They accept 'scutage'

▲ *A battle scene at the walls of Jerusalem.*

(payment) in lieu of feudal military service, and use the money to pay soldiers.

1128 The Council of Troyes approves the rule of the military brotherhood of the Knights Templar.

1130 Pope Innocent II bans tournaments.

*c.***1130** The earliest of the *chansons de geste*, *The Song of Roland* was written by this date, but may have been in circulation as early as 1050.

1135–39 Geoffrey of Monmouth's *History of the Kings of Britain* establishes Arthurian legend. Arthur was celebrated in Welsh poems as early as the 6th century AD.

1139 Pope Innocent II condemns 'the deadly art, which God hates, of cross-bowmen and archers'.

1140 Roger II, Norman King of Sicily, forbids the knighting of men who are liable to disturb the peace.

1142 The Spanish *Song of My Cid* is written down, but has been current in oral form for decades.

1147 Troops setting out on the Second Crusade stop in Portugal and capture Lisbon from its Muslim rulers.

1147–49 The Second Crusade is a failure.

1152 A German decree excludes peasants from being knights.

*c.***1160** Benoit de Sainte-Maure writes *The Romance of Troy*, establishing a genre, the *romans d'antiquités*, of poems of the feudal age featuring classical warriors.

*c.***1160** The French romance *Floire and Blancheflor* tells of the love between a Saracen knight and a Christian lady.

1170–91 French poet Chrétien de Troyes writes five Arthurian romances. They introduce the character of Sir Perceval and the theme of the quest for the Holy Grail.

1186 Holy Roman Emperor Frederick I bans the sons of peasants and the sons of priests from being knighted.

1189–92 The Third Crusade. Also known as the Kings' Crusade: Kings Richard I of England and Philip II of France and Holy Roman Emperor Frederick I all take part.

1194 King Richard I of England defies the papal ban and introduces a licensing system under which tournaments can be legally held in England.

*c.***1200** Norman poet Alexander of Bernay writes *The Alexander Romance*, about the Macedonian king Alexander the Great.

*c.***1200** The great German epic poem *The Song of the Nibelungs* is written.

*c.***1200–1220** German poet Wolfram von Eschenbach writes his masterpiece *Parzival*, a version of the Sir Perceval story.

1202–04 The Fourth Crusade attacks Zara (Hungary) and Constantinople.

1209–1229 The Catholic Church fights the Albigensian Crusade against the heretical Cathars of Occitania (southern France).

1212 The Children's Crusade. A tiny minority reach the Holy Land.

*c.***1215** German poet Gottfried von Strassburg writes *Tristan und Isolt*, a version of the story of Arthurian knight Tristan and Irish princess Iseult.

1217–21 The Fifth Crusade attacks Muslim Egypt but ends in failure.

1223 A 'Round Table' tournament at which knights act out the parts of King Arthur and his knights is held by John of Ibelin, Lord of Beirut, in Cyprus.

*c.*1225 French poem *The Order of Chivalry* describes an idealized knighting ceremony.

*c.*1225 Anglo-Norman poem *The History of William Marshal* celebrates the life of the great English knight (1146–1219).

1228–29 Largely through diplomacy rather than fighting, Holy Roman Emperor Frederick II gains Jerusalem, Nazareth and Bethlehem on the Sixth Crusade.

1235 The Cortes of Catalonia declares that only the sons of knights can be knighted.

1248–54 The Seventh Crusade, led by Louis IX of France, attacks Egypt.

*c.*1250 The Anglo-Norman *Romance of Richard Coeur de Lion* is written. Just 50 years after his death in 1199 , Richard I of England is a figure of legend.

*c.*1260 *The Golden Legend* by Jacobus de Voragine popularizes the story of St George and the dragon.

1270 Louis IX leads the Eighth Crusade against Muslim North Africa. He dies in Tunis and the crusade fails.

1271–72 Prince Edward of England leads the Ninth Crusade but achieves little.

1265 Majorcan poet and philosopher Ramon Llull writes the *Book of the Order of Chivalry*, a handbook for knights.

1278 A lavish Arthurian tournament is held at Le Hem, Picardy. It is described in the poem *The Book of Le Hem* by Anglo-Norman trouvère Sarrasin.

1285–1314 King Philip IV of France (r.1285–1314) has a considerable part of his army in paid rather than feudal service.

1303 The Catalan Company founded by Italian adventurer Roger de Flor is among the first groups of mercenary knights.

1312 The *chanson de geste*, *A Peacock's Vows* introduces the 'Nine Worthies' of chivalry. These are: three biblical figures – Joshua, David and Judas Maccabeus; three classical warriors – Hector of Troy, Alexander the Great and Julius Caesar; and three of the Christian era – Arthur, Charlemagne and Godfrey of Bouillon.

1316 The papal ban on tournaments is lifted by Pope John XXII.

1325 King Charles of Hungary establishes the Order of St George.

1326 The city of Florence acquires two cannon for its defences. This is the first known record of artillery guns in Europe.

*c.*1330 The first plate armour suits appear.

1332 King Alfonso XI of Castile and Leon (r.1312–50) establishes the Order of the Sash brotherhood of knights.

*c.*1335 The chivalric Order of St Catherine is formed in the Dauphiné, France.

1337–1453 The armies in the Hundred Years War contain many paid soldiers. They are mainly infantry and bowmen rather than knights, although Charles VII of France has 1500 cavalry on fixed pay.

23 Apr 1348 King Edward III of England and his son form the chivalric order of the Most Noble Order of the Garter.

*c.*1350 French knight Geoffroi de Charny writes the *Book of Chivalry*.

*c.*1350 Another company of mercenary knights, the Grand Company, is formed.

1351 In the celebrated 'Combat of the Thirty', two teams of thirty knights joust in Brittany.

1352 The French chivalric order, The Order of the Star is formed.

1356 The English defeat the French at Poitiers; in this victory, and at Crécy, knights are deployed to fight on foot.

1364 At the Battle of Auray English knight Sir John Chandos captures the great French knight Bertrand du Guesclin.

▼ *The battle of Crecy, 1346, with Edward the Black Prince in the centre.*

1367 Chandos, and Edward the Black Prince, take du Guesclin captive a second time. He is ransomed for 100,000 francs.

1369–1400 French poet and historian Jean Froissart writes his *Chronicles*, one of the most important sources on chivalry.

1382–87 Provençal writer Honoré Bonet composes *The Tree of Battles*.

1390 In the Jousts of St Inglevert in northern France four French knights occupy the lists for 30 days and fight all-comers.

1399 French knight Marshal de Boucicaut founds the order of the Enterprise of the Green Shield of the White Lady, with 12 members, sworn to protect women.

*c.*1400 The tilt or central barrier on the tournament lists is in common use from about this date.

1430 Philip the Good, Duke of Burgundy, establishes the chivalric Order of the Golden Fleece.

1434 Duarte, King of Portugal, writes *The Art of Good Horsemanship*, a manual on jousting and managing horses.

*c.*1450 René I of Naples, known as René d'Anjou, writes *The Book of Tournaments*.

*c.*1450 The first state infantry regiments are formed in France, part of a general movement at the time towards the establishment of professional standing armies.

1485 Sir Thomas Malory's *Le Morte d'Arthur*, one of the great English sources for the Arthurian tradition, is published.

1495 Matteo Maria Boiardo's *Orlando Innamorato* ('Roland in Love') is published.

1513–18 Italian courtier and diplomat Baldassare Castiglione writes *The Courtier*, a guide to being a gentleman, part of a movement away from chivalry to courtesy.

1515 French knight Pierre de Terrail, also known as the Chevalier de Bayard, knights his king, Francis I, after the Battle of Marignano.

1516 Lodovico Ariosto's *Orlando Furioso* ('Roland Maddened') is published.

1520 Kings Francis I of France and Henry VIII of England host the Field of the Cloth of Gold. Entertainments included jousting and wrestling and feasting.

1559 King Henry II of France sustains a fatal injury while jousting in Paris.

CHAPTER ONE

THE ORIGINS OF KNIGHTHOOD

In 732AD near Tours in what is now western France, the army of the Franks, commanded by the redoubtable Charles Martel, won a famous victory over a great Muslim force commanded by Abdul Rahman Al Ghafiqi. The Muslim army, with its powerful cavalry, was carrying out the largest in a series of northward invasions from the Umayyad Caliphate, an Islamic territory established in what is now Spain after an invasion from north Africa in 711. After this defeat, the Muslims abandoned all hope of invading northern Europe and settled in the Iberian peninsula, where their descendants lived until 1492.

The Battle of Tours has also been celebrated as a key stage in the history of chivalry, because it helped to establish the power of the Franks, whose heavy cavalry would be such an effective military tool in the hands of Charlemagne, King of the Franks 768–814, and because its demonstration of the steadfast bravery of Christian warriors fighting a great Islamic army struck a strong chord with audiences of the crusading era in the 11th century and afterwards.

Yet the Battle of Tours was not won by the Frankish cavalry. Charles Martel ordered his cavalry to dismount and fight alongside his infantry in a square. There, as footsoldiers, they stood firm in the face of repeated charges by the Islamic cavalry – in the words of the Muslim Mozarabic Chronicle 'unmoving as a solid wall, holding fast like a great ice block'.

▲ *Emperor Charlemagne leads his knights into battle in Agolant, Spain.*

◄ *The Battle of Tours in AD732 was a defining moment in European history, and can perhaps be seen as the conception of knighthood.*

THE WORLD BEFORE KNIGHTS

EARLY MOUNTED WARRIORS

Knights of the Middle Ages were not the first warriors to ride into battle on horseback, nor were their predecessors the mounted cavalry of the Franks. The use of horses in war extends back thousands of years, almost into prehistory.

PRECURSORS OF THE CAVALRY

People may have tamed and begun to ride the horse as long ago as 4000BC. We know that as far back as the 2nd millennium BC warriors fought in horse-drawn chariots: the Indo-Iranian nomads who overran the ancient civilization of northern India and Pakistan in c.1500BC fought with war chariots and iron weapons. The use of the war chariot was invented in the homeland of the Indo-Iranian peoples, probably the steppes of Central Asia, and they spread its use as they fanned out in at least two waves of migration from their original

▼ *Between the 9th and 7th centuries BC, the Assyrian cavalry were famed for their speed and strength in combat. They were armed with bows and arrows and spears.*

homeland in c.1500BC and c.800BC. The chariots were adopted in the Assyrian, Babylonian and ancient Egyptian empires.

In the 9th century BC the Assyrian army had a powerful cavalry. The Assyrian mounted warriors fought principally with bows and arrows, although they also carried shields and swords. They rode without the benefit of saddles, stirrups or spurs. The warriors needed to be highly skilled riders because handling weapons while moving at speed on horseback was an extremely demanding task. They rode in pairs, taking it in turns to hold the reins of both horses, while the other prepared his bow and fired an arrow.

From the 5th to 3rd century BC the Scythians – originally another group of Indo-Iranian steppe nomads – were famed for their prowess as mounted warriors. Like the Assyrians, they rode bareback, fighting with bows and arrows. The Scythians were truly bloodthirsty fighters who beheaded and scalped any warriors they caught, scraped out the skulls and used the hollowed bone as a drinking cup.

▲ *With the help of his cavalry squadrons, the Macedonian king Alexander – known to history as 'the Great' – built a vast empire.*

ALEXANDER'S COMPANIONS

The armies of ancient Greece relied principally on infantry, but cavalry was a key part of the army of Alexander the Great, the 4th-century BC Macedonian king. He achieved extraordinary conquests and would later become a celebrated figure in medieval chivalric romances.

Alexander's cavalry was strikingly similar to the cadre of noble knights who fought alongside their lord in the Middle Ages. The main component of cavalry in Alexander's army was an aristocratic elite called the *hetairoi* (companions), equipped with a long spear for mounted combat and a slashing sword and a straight sword to use if they were forced to dismount. They also wore a helmet and a linen or bronze cuirass (protective jacket).

Alexander rode into battle at the head of his companions when they charged. He would use his infantry to immobilize the enemy and then attack with the companions on the enemy's right flank or from behind, while another lesser group of cavalry attacked on the left.

THE CATAPHRACT

The mounted soldiers of the Parthian empire, at its height in the 1st century BC, struck fear into the hearts of their enemies, including the armies of Ancient Rome. The mounted Parthian warriors rode armoured steeds and were famous for firing arrows over their shoulders as they rode away – a tactic known ever afterwards as the 'Parthian shot'. The Parthians – and their successors, the Seleucid and Sassanid empires of Iran – also used small units of armed cavalry fighting with lances, a formation called *kataphraktos* ('protected by a barrier') in Greek, and which came to be more commonly known as the 'cataphract'.

The Roman army also had cavalry. In the early years of the Roman republic, the cavalry was filled by wealthy landowners, the *equites*, who could afford a horse as well as the necessary weapons, but increasingly the *equites* became an elite social group and the cavalry was filled with foreign fighters from the tribes of the Iberians, Gauls and Numidians (Berber tribesmen from northern Africa). For a long period the Roman cavalry was used mainly for scouting and skirmishing rather than as an arm of the military in battle. However, during the Battle of Carrhae

▼ *Mounted warriors in the Persian army sat on large, coloured blankets. They did not wear armour or carry shields.*

(modern Harran, Turkey) in 53BC, where Roman general Crassus was humiliatingly defeated by the Parthian general Spahbod Surena, the Romans saw how effectively large groups of cavalry – especially lance-bearing cataphracts – could be used in war. Thereafter they used more cavalry with better-trained men and began to deploy cataphracts of their own.

GOTHIC HORSEMEN

As the Roman Empire collapsed in the west in the 5th century AD, a number of Germanic tribes prospered in Europe. The Goths and Vandals who sacked Rome used powerful cavalry. A little earlier, at the Battle of Adrianople (modern Edirne, Turkey) in AD378, the Gothic cavalry had imposed a devastating defeat on the Roman army. This battle is traditionally seen as one of the first great triumphs for heavy cavalry and also as the conflict that initiated the final collapse of the Roman Empire in the west.

In the eastern Roman Empire, based on Constantinople (modern Istanbul), heavy cavalry became an important part of the imperial army. Under the command of Flavius Belisarius, 6th-century general to

▲ *The ancient Roman army combined the speed of lance-bearing horsemen with the tenacity of legionary footsoldiers.*

Byzantine Emperor Justinian I, bands of heavy cavalry were a powerful weapon, fighting with javelins, bows and arrows.

In Europe, too, the use of armed cavalry spread. The Franks, a Germanic tribe who took control of most of the former Roman colony of Gaul and who would serve as highly effective mounted warriors under Charlemagne, initially fought on foot. They learned the use of cavalry from the Goths and many years later would pass it on to the Vikings – whose descendants, the Normans, were such accomplished practitioners of cavalry warfare.

By the time of the Battle of Tours in 732 the Franks were beginning to ride horses to war. The horses they used were little better than carthorses and their principal effectiveness was as beasts of burden rather than fighting animals. Wealthier Franks would ride horses to battle, then dismount to fight. They would be fresher for battle than their enemies, who might have marched for many days to reach the battlefield.

FEUDAL WARRIORS
THE RISE OF THE FRANKS AND THE EARLY FEUDAL SYSTEM

The nobles who fought in the heavy cavalry of Charlemagne, King of the Franks (r. 768–814), served their monarch in times of war in a way that prefigured the bonds of medieval knights to their lord. The Frankish nobles were tied to their lord by an early form of the feudal system, in which they were granted land in return for military service.

THE EMERGENCE OF THE FRANKS
The Franks were a federation of Germanic tribes, first known in history as settlers on the east bank of the Lower Rhine river in the 3rd century AD. They gained former Roman territories in what is now Belgium in the mid-4th century, and some of their leaders became allies of Rome, acting as guards of the empire's frontiers. They were already known as redoubtable warriors, and many of them served as auxiliaries in the Roman army.

▼ *The baptism of King Clovis by Bishop Remigius of Reims in 496 began the Franks' long association with the Catholic Church. The 6th-century historian Gregory of Tours likened Clovis to the biblical King David as father of his people and faith.*

▲ *Pepin III, son of Charles Martel and father of Charlemagne, was crowned by Pope Boniface I in 751. He was the first Frankish king to receive papal blessing.*

During the 5th century, as Rome's hold on its empire in Europe grew weaker, the Franks took control of north-eastern parts of the former Roman colony of Gaul (modern France). Clovis I (r. 481–511), king of the Salian Franks, one branch of the Frankish federation, conquered the rival groups, uniting all the Franks as he built an empire encompassing all of Gaul, save Burgundy and what is now Provence. He founded the Merovingian line of kings (named after his grandfather Merovech) that ruled until the rise of the Carolingian kings of the Franks in 751.

A CATHOLIC PRINCE
Clovis I also began the Franks' long association with the Catholic Church, converting to Catholic Christianity on his marriage to a Catholic Burgundian princess, Clotilde. At this time many other Germanic tribes had converted to the Arian form of Christianity (named after 4th-century theologian, Arius), which held that Christ was a created being rather than an equal presence with God the Father from the beginning of all things. Arianism was generally viewed as a heresy. However, the Franks, following the example of their leader, converted in large numbers from their pagan beliefs to Catholicism. Because

he united the Frankish tribes and the territories of Gaul, Clovis is often celebrated as the founder of France.

Following his death in 511, however, inheritance disputes broke up the Frankish empire into a number of competing kingdoms. The authority of the Merovingian kings withered and then power resided increasingly in the hand of the *Major Palatii* ('Mayor of the Palace') in each kingdom. This position had arisen from one current in the Roman Empire, that of *Major Domus* ('Household Supervisor') appointed by landowners to manage a number of estates.

RENEWED EXPANSION OF THE FRANKS
In the late 7th century, Pépin, Mayor of the Palace in the Frankish kingdom of Austrasia (the north-east part of the former empire), embarked on a campaign

---

COMMENDATION
A vassal swore loyalty in a special ceremony called the 'commendation'. The vassal knelt and put both his hands in those of the lord as he swore the oath of fealty, promising to be loyal to the lord and to provide military or other service, such as farming land. The lord kissed his vassal and pulled him to his feet. He handed him a symbol of the agreement – sometimes a piece of earth. The vassal was granted the lord's protection – an important consideration at a time when central authority was often weak and raiders such as the Vikings were at large. In early times the vassal might become part of the lord's retinue, but by the 9th century the oath required the vassal to provide mounted military service with lance, shield and sword.

▲ *The Frankish empire, initially won on the battlefield, was subsequently fractured by war. Charlemagne's grandson Lothair I was crowned emperor by Pope Paschal I in 823, and expected to inherit, but military defeats forced him to share power with his brothers.*

of territorial expansion. He took control of the neighbouring kingdom of Neustria (the north-west part of the former empire) and defeated the Frisians to the north of Austrasia. On Pépin's death in 714, his illegitimate son, Charles, succeeded as mayor and continued Frankish expansion. His military exploits won him a resounding reputation as Charles Martel ('the Hammer'). It was he who in 732 stopped the northward expansion of Islamic warriors at the bruising Battle of Tours.

VASSALAGE AND EARLY FORMS OF FEUDALISM

The principle in Frankish territories was that every free Frank was required to fight for the king. In addition Frankish kings kept groups of sworn warriors, called *antrustiones,* or vassals. These men swore loyalty to the ruler and promised him military service; in return they could expect to be equipped and fed, and would receive a share of war plunder. This arrangement had grown out of the *comitatus,* a group of sworn warriors serving and fighting for a leader in Germanic tribes. The antrustiones were given leading administrative positions as a *comes* (count) and military positions as a *dux* (duke).

In the 8th century, trade and an economy based on money had broken down in the Frankish territories, and wealth was measured in land. The principal landholders were the king, the Church and Frankish lords, to whom the king delegated control of sections of territory. The kings parcelled out land in the form of a benefice, a grant of full ownership for the lifetime of the recipient.

Under the Frankish kings the granting of benefices came to be associated with vassalage in the form of the fiefdom: the land given to the vassal remained the king's but rights over it were granted to the vassals in return for an oath of lifelong loyalty to the lord and the promise of military service.

The fiefdom tied to sworn military service became the basis of the feudal system that structured early medieval society. The lord–vassal relationship could be found at all social levels: between the king and his leading counts and dukes; between these men and the tenants on their land; and equally further down between the holder of a small fief and the vassals who held sections of his smallholding.

It became customary for the holders of fiefdoms to be able to bequeath them to their sons, and the holding of land in the form of the inheritable fiefdom allowed noble families to gradually build up considerable territories and pass them on after death. Some families became so powerful that they could begin to challenge the authority of the king. The right of holders of fiefdoms to pass the land on to their sons was accepted, but not legal until Charlemagne's grandson, King Charles the Bald, decreed that if a count died when the king was away on campaign, the count's son could inherit.

▼ *Charles Martel was impressed by Muslim horsemen at the Battle of Tours. He set about strengthening the Frankish cavalry, taking Church land and distributing it among his sworn followers to increase the number of landowners wealthy enough to equip themselves as mounted warriors.*

A CHRISTIAN EMPIRE IN EUROPE
THE HOLY ROMAN EMPIRE OF CHARLEMAGNE

Charles Martel's descendants – notably his grandson, Charles I, King of the Franks from AD768 – created a great empire that encompassed much of western and central Europe. They allied themselves with the Christian Church, and accepted the blessing of the pope in Rome on their rule, and through their conquests spread the faith, imposing Christianity on pagan tribes such as the Saxons in what is now northern Germany.

The Frankish armies built their success on the exploits of a highly mobile, well-equipped cavalry. Charles I was known as Charles the Great, in Latin *Carolus Magnus* and therefore as Charlemagne.

THE CAROLINGIAN DYNASTY
Charles Martel had ruled as king in all but name: he was Mayor of the Palace, and nominally subject to the Merovingian kings, descendants of Clovis I. In 751, however, Martel's son Pépin the Short ousted the last of the Merovingians, Childeric III, and became king in his own right. He founded the Carolingian dynasty (named from the Latin form of Charles, *Carolus*, in honour of his father Charles Martel and his son, Charlemagne).

Pépin was anointed twice, first by the Christian missionary St Boniface and then in 754, together with his two sons Carloman and Charlemagne, by Pope Stephen II in a magnificent ceremony at the Saint Denis Basilica in Paris. Pépin defeated the Lombards of northern Italy, and gave territories he had won to the papacy. He also brought Aquitaine (southwestern France) into the Frankish realm. He was succeeded by his sons in 768, but when Carloman died in 771, Charlemagne ruled alone.

CHRISTIAN WARRIORS
One of Charlemagne's first campaigns was to invade once more the kingdom of the Lombards in northern Italy, where

▲ *The papacy supported the rise of Frankish power. Charlemagne seized control in northern Italy in 774 and had his rule blessed by Pope Adrian I in Milan.*

Carloman's widow had fled seeking help. Charlemagne defeated and deposed the Lombard king, Desiderius, and seized the crown for himself in 774. He took possession of his nephews, who had a claim to power via their father, and they subsequently disappeared – presumably disposed of. He appointed Frankish lords to key positions in the Lombards' territory. In the course of this campaign he celebrated Easter in Rome with the pope and reaffirmed the alliance between the Franks and the papacy.

The association of Frankish rule with the Catholic Church was a crucial element in the development of knighthood. The mounted warriors of Charlemagne's army fought in the name of Christ. The Church developed theories under which violence could be seen as holy if committed in a sacred cause.

FIGHTING FOR CHRIST
Charlemagne saw it as a king's duty to spread the Christian faith. He rode into battle with an elite cadre of mounted warriors to fight for the Cross. In 772 he launched an attack on the pagan Saxons, a fiercely independent Germanic group, rivals to the Franks, in an attempt to bring them within his Christian realm. The Saxons proved to be of stern stuff: Charlemagne's onslaught against them lasted on and off for 32 years, until 804. He led no fewer than 18 campaigns himself at the head of his elite unit of soldiers.

He must have thought he was close to his goal when he oversaw a series of mass baptisms of Saxons in 775–77, but despite signing a treaty of allegiance in 777 the Saxons rebelled again, and Charlemagne unleashed a terrible punishment in the mass execution in 782 of no fewer than 4,500 Saxons. In the course of his reign he succeeded in bending all the other Germanic tribes to his will – defeating the Bavarians, the Frisians, the Alemanni and the Thuringians.

DEFEAT AND CHRISTIANIZATION OF THE AVARS

In the late 790s Charlemagne launched an onslaught on the Avars, a nomadic tribe from Asia who had settled in what is now Hungary and had launched raids into the eastern part of the Frankish realm. (The Avars were called 'Huns' by Charlemagne's biographer Einhard.) Charlemagne personally led a devastating rout of the Avars in 790–91. Further campaigns led by Charlemagne's second son Pépin (known as Pépin of Italy) and Duke Eric of Friull defeated the Avars decisively, and their leaders submitted, swearing fealty to Charlemagne as his vassals and accepting his Christian faith.

THE WESTERN ROMAN EMPIRE REVIVED

Charlemagne set out at first to maintain good relations with both the pope in Rome and the rulers of the Byzantine or eastern Roman empire in Constantinople. He was in Rome once more in 781, for the anointing of his sons Pépin and Louis as kings of the Lombards and of the

▼ *Christian warriors led by Charlemagne were overcome by Muslims in the Battle of Roncesvalles in Spain (778). The defeat was treated elegiacally in the* Song of Roland.

Aquitanians respectively. He recognized the Byzantine empress Irene – and the two rulers even entered into negotiations for the arranged marriage of Charlemagne's daughter Rotrude to Irene's son (the future Byzantine emperor Constantine VI) but the negotiations failed and the arrangement was broken off.

In 799 he gave refuge to Pope Leo III who had fled a revolt by Italian nobles; Charlemagne had him escorted safely back

▲ *The chapel of Charlemagne's imperial palace, built in c.790, survives as part of Aachen cathedral (now in Germany).*

to Rome. The following year, Charlemagne visited Rome and Leo crowned him 'August Emperor'. This was an attempt to revive the Roman Empire in the west as a Christian realm.

It was a challenge to the Byzantine Empire, for nominally the popes and the Franks were subjects of the eastern empire, and the Byzantine emperor was seen as the ruler of all Christians. Briefly it seemed possible that the two halves of the empire might be reunited: Charlemagne proposed marriage to Empress Irene, but the negotiations failed and she died in 802. Subsequently there was a stand-off, and then the two sides fought an intermittent war over Byzantine-held territories in Italy. Finally in 812 Byzantine emperor Michael I recognized Charlemagne as emperor under the title of *Imperator Romanorum gubernans imperium* ('Emperor governing the lands of the Romans'). The following year Charlemagne declared his son Louis to be co-emperor and his chosen successor. Charlemagne himself died in 814.

PARAGON OF CHIVALRY

CHARLEMAGNE THE GREAT

In medieval Europe Charlemagne was seen as the model Christian king or emperor. A superb military tactician, he marshalled large armies and made effective use of the power of mounted warriors with his cavalry. He rode into battle with his elite cadre of mounted warriors, in whom medieval knights saw their forerunners. He was a Christian warrior, who fought to spread the faith of Christ: all the peoples he defeated accepted Christianity as part of their submission. Centuries later, he was celebrated as a chivalric hero in *chansons de geste* (chivalric poems) and a perfect knight, perhaps history's first great exemplar of the chivalric code.

CHARLEMAGNE'S FAITH

In his early campaign of AD774 against the Lombards, when he deposed the Lombard king Desiderius, took the crown for himself, eliminated his brother's sons as

▼ *Charlemagne attends Mass while on campaign. The wars he waged against pagan Germanic tribes were fought in Christ's name to spread the Gospel.*

potential rivals and renewed the Franks' alliance with the pope, Charlemagne demonstrated several of his key qualities: strategic intelligence, decisiveness, military force, and an element of ruthlessness in negating the claim to power of his nephews. The events of 774 also demonstrated his combination of political manoeuvring and religious faith – for while his alliance with the papacy was politically expedient, his commitment to the Christian faith was genuine.

Charlemagne was driven by a desire for power, but he believed himself to be doing God's will. He did not accept that the pope had any sovereignty over him: in his laws he described himself as *Imperator a Deo Coronatus* ('Emperor Crowned by God'), indicating that he was subject only to God.

AT COURT AND AS A PATRON

Not least among the qualities that contributed to Charlemagne's enduring reputation in the Middle Ages was his commitment to the Church and to learning. He was a great patron of the Church and of education and oversaw a revival of

art and learning known to history as the 'Carolingian Renaissance'.

He gathered many of the great minds of contemporary Europe at his court in Aachen, among them the Anglo-Saxon monk Alcuin who reorganized education within Charlemagne's vast realms. Alcuin reintroduced the study of the seven liberal arts of music, astronomy, geometry, logic, arithmetic, grammar and rhetoric, which had been studied in ancient Rome.

Another key figure among the courtiers at Aachen was the monk Einhard, originally a pupil of Alcuin, who wrote a biography of the emperor. From Einhard's account, we know that Charlemagne was well-built and unusually tall – his height was noted to be seven times the length of his feet. He had large eyes and nose, a full head of grey hair and a cheerful face. He walked purposefully and spoke with a higher voice than an observer might expect. From other sources we know that although he had rough manners, he enjoyed debating with the learned men he had gathered around him and was always keen to learn.

A FAMOUS DEFEAT IN SPAIN

Under Charlemagne, the Frankish army was a military machine of awesome effectiveness. Yet one of the great *chansons de geste* that celebrated medieval chivalric heroes focused on a rare defeat for this warrior king.

This setback took place in the Pyrenees mountains in 778. Charlemagne had invaded northern Spain at the urging of some Muslim emissaries whose request for help against the Umayyad emir of Córdoba had appealed to him as an opportunity to add lustre to his military reputation while also expanding the reach of Christianity into largely Muslim Spain. The campaign, during which he besieged and failed to capture Zaragoza, was not a success, but worse was to follow – for, as

▲ *Charlemagne refused to accept that his power was dependent upon papal approval. To emphasize this, he used the words 'Emperor Crowned by God' in his laws.*

he led his army back through the Pyrenees, they were ambushed by Basque fighters (perhaps in alliance with Muslim warriors) and many in Charlemagne's army were killed. One of these was Hroudland or Roland, Warden of the border territories with Brittany, and the warrior who gave his name to the 11th-century epic poem the *Chanson de Roland* (the *Song of Roland*), a masterpiece of medieval literature that makes a great celebration of this defeat.

CHARLEMAGNE THE WARRIOR

We know plenty about Charlemagne's campaigns, his political manoeuvring and his commitment to education, but we have little certain information about him as a warrior. Yet this aspect of his life was important in the Middle Ages, when he was revered as a knight, and in works such as the *Song of Roland* his relationship with his elite companions in his cavalry was presented as the epitome of chivalry, the perfection of chivalric relationship between a lord and his knights.

We do, however, have a description of Charlemagne dressed for battle. Notker of St Gall, a 9th-century Benedictine monk at the Abbey of St Gall (at modern St Gallen, Switzerland), left in his work *Gesta Caroli Magni* (*Life of Charlemagne*) a description of the king equipped for the battlefield. It refers to him as 'the Iron King': saying that his armour consisted of an iron helm, with sleeves of iron armour and a chain mail tunic; his upper legs also were covered with chain mail, with iron greaves on the lower leg.

KING WITH KNIGHTLY VIRTUES

Totila, King of the Ostrogoths in the mid-6th century, was celebrated as a great early precursor of chivalry in much the same way as Charlemagne was seen as an early example of the ideal knight. In the 540s Totila recaptured for the Goths most of central and southern Italy, which had been taken by the Byzantine or eastern Roman Empire. In near contemporary accounts, Totila was celebrated for his humanity and fairness in dealing with defeated enemies – later important chivalric virtues. He was also a great mounted warrior and a figure of heroic appearance. The 6th-century Byzantine historian Procopius described Totila's magnificent attire: gold armour, with adornments hanging from the cheek pieces, and a purple helmet and lance. He also praised the king's horsemanship and weapon-handling: in front of the armies arrayed on the field of battle, he danced on his horse and was able to throw and catch his spear while parading on horseback. Totila's name was Baduila, but chronicles suggest he fought under the name Totila.

▼ *On 21 March 543 Totila paid a visit at Monte Cassino to Benedict of Nursia, founder of the Benedictine monastic rule. Three years later, Totila took Rome.*

THE EMPEROR'S CAVALRY
MOUNTED WARRIORS IN THE CAROLINGIAN ARMY

Charlemagne's triumphant military success depended on his use of very large, well-equipped and superbly disciplined armies. They contained a large contingent of light cavalry and a smaller elite section of heavy cavalry. Some estimates of the number of mounted warriors in the Frankish army go as high as 35,000 men. Charlemagne issued detailed edicts laying out requirements for how the armies should be raised, equipped and supplied with food and weapons.

A MILITARY MACHINE

Charlemagne was a great tactician, but a major part of his armies' effectiveness depended on organization. Many of his army manoeuvres were only possible because his military machine was so big and so well organized that he was able to keep two or more large armies in the field at once.

As well as fighting on more than one front at once, his armies could undertake long-range campaigns of conquest – beyond the river Rhine, across the Alps in

▼ *A bearded, regal Charlemagne elevates a warrior to the cavalry. The illustration is from the 14th century and is coloured by notions of chivalry from this later age.*

Italy, in the far west of Brittany and once even across the Pyrenees in northern Spain (although this campaign was the scene of the celebrated failure in the Pass of Roncesvalles). In battle Charlemagne's armies were large enough to split into separate units. It was a favourite tactic of his – used in 778 in Spain, in 787 in Bavaria and in 791 in Pannonia – to outflank the enemy with columns of troops.

Charlemagne did not usually wage war during the winter. His custom was to gather his army at Easter, prior to embarking on campaigns in the summer months. Sometimes, however, he remained in the territory he was intent on subjugating for

▲ *Wearing the typical conical helmets of the day, mounted warriors in Charlemagne's army follow the baggage train on campaign.*

the winter break. In 776, for example, he defeated the Saxons at Lippespringe and forcibly baptized them, but they rose up in revolt, throwing off the Christian faith which they had accepted, almost at once. That winter he kept his court in Saxony – and, unusually, he kept up regular raids against Saxon targets during the winter months.

RAISING AN ARMY

Each count was held responsible for bringing with him all the warriors who were his vassals – save four, whom he could leave behind to guard his property and protect his wife. Bishops and abbots also had to give military service, with all their vassals – although they, too, could leave a pair of warriors to protect their possessions. A royal vassal at court did not have to perform military service, but he was responsible for ensuring that all his vassals joined up.

During the course of Charlemagne's reign, selective service became accepted: three vassals might join together to equip a fourth, who would go on campaign. One of the emperor's edicts, issued in Saxony in 806, required five Saxons to equip a sixth to fight for the king in a projected Spanish campaign, and for two more men to equip another warrior to serve in Bohemia.

Charlemagne's armies were always well supplied, and his campaigns were usually well planned. He ordered his mounted warriors to bring three months' worth of food and six months' worth of military clothing and weapons. The decree even specified that these three months would begin when the army assembled on campaign rather than when the warriors embarked from their homes. Herds of livestock for food were part of an army's baggage train.

During the Saxon campaigns the troops were well enough equipped to build bridges and forts; the army had collapsible boats for crossing the river Ebro on the Spanish campaign of 778 and carried a moveable bridge for its 792 campaign against the Avars. When he had forces fighting simultaneously in Hungary and Saxony he tried – though without success – to dig a canal between the Danube and the Rhine.

▼ *Charlemagne's forces fight at Pamplona, Spain, during the ill-fated campaign that ended in defeat in the Pass of Roncesvalles.*

FORTS AND PLUNDER

In conquered territories he ordered the building of permanent garrisoned fortifications – forerunners of the castles built by medieval knights. Plundering enemy riches was an accepted part of campaigning. The campaign against the Avars in 790–91 produced so much booty that 15 wagons were needed to carry it back to the court at Aachen.

Discipline was strict. Drunkenness was officially forbidden. There was a stiff fine for those who failed to attend when required. Desertion was punished with seizing all of a warrior's property followed by execution.

EQUIPMENT AND WEAPONS

Charlemagne laid down strict requirements for the military equipment his troops should have. In 792 his edict required mounted warriors to have a lance, a shield and both long and short swords, in addition to a horse. In 802 the warriors were ordered to bring body armour as well. In 805 he decreed that each mounted soldier in possession of at

▲ *Fighting beneath a heavenly apparition of the Cross, Charlemagne's cavalry and the sheer might of his army defeat the pagan Avars, who were superbly skilled horsemen themselves, near the river Danube in 791.*

least 300 acres (121 hectares) had to bring a *byrnie* (tunic of chain mail). The decree also stated that warriors who had chain mail armour but did not bring it to battle risked punishment by losing their fiefdom.

A typical mounted warrior in one of Charlemagne's armies had a chain mail tunic that extended down to his knees and was slit at the side to allow greater ease of movement. Some had a scale overshirt instead – a jacket of leather or fabric with metal or horn pieces attached to it. The warrior wore a conical helmet and carried a round shield with a spike in the centre, so that it could be used as a thrusting weapon as well as for defence. He had a long lance, used for thrusting – in this era, groups of mounted warriors did not yet charge with couched lance. His sword had a rounded end, and was effective for cutting but not for stabbing.

A TIME OF UNREST

THE PROTECTIVE ROLE OF MOUNTED WARRIORS IN AN UNRULY WORLD

In the years after Charlemagne's death in 814 his empire swiftly disintegrated in power struggles among his sons and their descendants. At the same time his former territories were assailed by violent raiders: from the north, Vikings came by sea and river in their longships; from the east, the reckless Magyars came on horseback; from the south and west (from North Africa and the Iberian Peninsula) came fierce Islamic raiders. It was a lawless time, seemingly lacking effective central authority.

Monasteries and churches were as much the raiders' targets as palaces and farms, and churchmen as well as lords looked to mounted warriors for protection. This led to the first idealizations of the warrior-horsemen as defenders of the Church and of right against lawless pagans. It was a key stage in the progression from the mounted warrior of Charlemagne's army to the knight of the 11th and 12th centuries, who was seen as a *miles Christi* ('soldier of Christ').

▼ *Viking attacks by sea were hard to defend against because their swift, powerful ships swept in, looted and departed before local defences could be organized.*

THE FIRST TRUE CAVALRY ENGAGEMENTS

Charlemagne's son Louis the Pious reigned for 26 years, 814–40. Early in his reign he attempted to settle the question of the succession among his descendants, but not to their satisfaction: he was twice deposed in major revolts by his sons, then subsequently reinstalled. After his death his three surviving sons fought amongst themselves, then divided the empire into three under the Treaty of Verdun (843). The former East Frankish kingdom became Francia Orientalis and was taken by Louis the German; the West Frankish kingdom became Francia Occidentalis, and was given to Charles the Bald. A central strip called Francia Media and the title of emperor was given to Lothair. (Francia Occidentalis and Francia Orientalis were later the basis of the countries of France and Germany respectively.)

These wars saw the first true mounted warrior engagements as cavalries from opposing armies met in full charge. By this stage the stirrup had been widely adopted, but the mounted warriors had not yet developed the technique of charging with couched lance.

A NEW WARRIOR CLASS

Power struggles continued for decades. All the time the authority and influence of the royal house grew weaker; meanwhile, Magyars and Vikings struck repeatedly. The most effective resistance came from local lords, whose power grew steadily as they built a large territorial holding, often through the grant by weak kings of hereditary fiefdoms. These lords in turn granted fiefdoms to their warrior supporters. An elite class of landholding warrior-knights began to develop.

These warriors' principal loyalty was to their lord rather than the king. In 792–93 Charlemagne had been able to impose an oath of loyalty to the king on all royal vassals and required the vassals to make their vassals swear it also. But as royal authority collapsed, and counts became more powerful as they accumulated land, it began to be accepted that vassals would fight for their lord against the king.

VIKING RAIDS AND CONSOLIDATING LOCAL POWER

From the 830s through to 910 Viking raids were a persistent threat to the western Frankish lands. They hit coastal targets

THE BATTLE OF AUGSBURG

King Otto I of the Germans unleashed heavy cavalry against the Magyar horsemen at the Battle of Augsburg on the river Lech in 955. Chronicle accounts claim that Otto's army numbered around 10,000 while the Magyars fielded 50,000 warriors, but modern historians believe that the true figures were perhaps 1,000 against 5,000. Initially the Magyars gained the upper hand, and appeared to have outflanked Otto's army, but many Magyars dismounted to begin looting the Frankish baggage train and Otto sent his knights to ride them down. The main part of the battle was marked by the disciplined charge of Otto's knights, who drove back and overwhelmed the Magyar horsemen, and then ruthlessly pursued them from the field – according to some accounts – for two days. The Magyars were routed, and never again raided Frankish territories; Otto's victory was hailed by contemporaries as a great triumph for Christian knights.

▲ *The Magyar mounted warriors were expert at ambushing troops, and often pretended to retreat before turning suddenly on their pursuers.*

as well as any settlements that could be reached by river. In *c*.840 they raided Nourmoutier, Utrecht and Antwerp; in 841 they razed Rouen; in 843 they attacked Nantes and sailed up the river Loire. By the 850s they had set up camps on the Seine, Loire and Garonne. In 847, 861 and 865 they attacked Paris.

Frankish kings relied on local counts and dukes to repel the threat. Charles the Bald of the western Frankish kingdom (r. 844–70) made fiefdoms hereditary as a means of maintaining the loyalty of local lords who had proved their worth in countering the Vikings. Local lords who benefited in this way included Baldwin 'Iron-Arm' who made his name combating the Vikings in Flanders and was made *margrave* (ruler) of Flanders by Charles the Bald in 864. Similarly Richard the Justiciar, who defeated the Vikings in

Burgundy in 888 and relieved the Viking siege of Chartres in 911, was established as the first margrave of Burgundy.

Raids on the western Frankish kingdom largely came to an end after the early 10th century, when a settlement of Vikings was established by Charles III the Simple in what became Normandy, as a buffer zone to protect against future raiding.

MAGYAR HORSEMEN

The Magyars were warlike descendants of nomadic people originally from the region of the Ural Mountains, who had settled in what is now Ukraine in *c*.830. They began launching mounted raids on the eastern Frankish territories in 862.

They were superb horsemen and archers, who fought mainly with bows and arrows but also with lassos and javelins. They would pour into an area,

looting widely, then disappear just as quickly. Otto I (r. 936–73) of the eastern Frankish kingdom (around this time generally described as Germany) ended the Magyar threat once and for all at the Battle of Ausgburg in 955 (see box).

WAR BY SEA

For much of the 9th century, Islamic raiders dominated the Mediterranean. They captured Bari in Italy, the island of Crete and part of Sicily (where they developed Palermo as a great cosmopolitan city). They established bases in what is now southern France, including Farakshanit (Fraxinet) near modern St Tropez, and raided up the river Rhone as far as Upper and Lower Burgundy.

The Europeans called them infidels (people of no faith) or Saracens from the Arabic word *sharqiyin* ('Easterners'). In southern France feudal lords defended local populations against the raiders, and achieved increasing independence from Frankish or Byzantine authority in building fortifications to hold the raiders at bay.

ALFRED THE GREAT AND ENGLISH MILITIAS
KNIGHTHOOD IN ENGLAND BEFORE THE NORMAN CONQUEST

Alfred of Wessex (r. 871–99) is the only king in English history to be honoured with the epithet 'the Great'. As with Charlemagne in Europe, Alfred has been revered by later generations in England as a great warrior monarch, military reformer, administrator, lawgiver and educator. Like Charlemagne, Alfred was a close ally of the Church, and celebrated as a defender and promoter of the Christian faith against pagan enemies. Throughout the age of chivalry he was celebrated as a pioneer of knightly virtues such as bravery, charity and magnanimity, as a giver of laws, and as an inspirational example of a king and general who achieved victory when all seemed lost.

MILITARY REFORMS
In 871 Anglo-Saxon England appeared to be at the mercy of Danish Vikings: a great Viking army had landed in 865 and won control of York, Northumbria and East

Anglia. Alfred, still a prince, led the armies of his brother King Aethelred of Wessex in a stirring victory over the Danes on the Ridgeway at Ashdown in Berkshire on 8 January 871. However, the Danes quickly regrouped afterwards and won important victories. Alfred meanwhile acceded to the throne on the death of Aethelred.

Alfred bought peace by bribing the invaders, but the Vikings, after conquering the Anglo-Saxon kingdom of Mercia, attacked again in 877, penetrating far into Wessex. Alfred fought back, initially conducting a guerrilla war from a base deep in the impenetrable wetlands of Somerset, then the following year leading a West Saxon army to another great victory over the Danes, in the Battle of Edington on Salisbury Plain. Alfred's men harried the Danes for more than 15 miles (24km) back to the invaders' base at Chippenham, which surrendered after a siege of 14 days. Alfred later freed London from the Danes.

The Viking leader Guthrum and his army pledged not to attack Wessex, but the invaders remained in England, established in the eastern region of the country, between the rivers Thames and Tees, in the area known as the Danelaw. Alfred set about improving his kingdom's defences and the effectiveness of its army. He split the *fyrd* (militia) into two, and thereafter ensured that one half was always ready for action while the other half rested at home. He adopted the tactics of the invaders, introducing mobile groups of mounted warriors as part of the army.

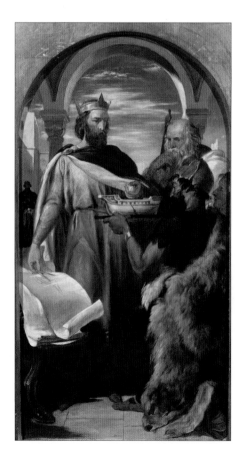

◄ *King Alfred discusses his new ship design with associates. The heavy boats, when made, ran aground on their first use.*

▶ *This iron ceremonial helmet was buried with an Anglo-Saxon chief at Sutton Hoo, Suffolk, in the 7th century. The Anglo-Saxon warriors were footsoldiers, but their army did use Celtic-British cavalry units.*

▲ *Alfred is a great figure in the traditions of English law as well as in the country's military history. His* Book of Laws *was based on three Saxon law codes.*

Alfred also revamped the navy and introduced a heavier, 60-oar boat that he had designed. Most importantly, he ordered the building of a string of defensive forts, or burghs, around his kingdom. He decreed that there should be a fort within 20 miles of every settlement. Some of the burghs were newly built, others were based on old Roman or Iron Age forts; some were small, others appear to have been planned from the start as fortified towns.

▲ *The two sides of a silver penny issued by King Alfred in c.880.*

NECESSARY KNOWLEDGE

Alfred believed that the violent visitations of the Vikings were God's judgement on an ignorant people, and saw it as his Christian duty to revive learning in the kingdom. Probably inspired by the example of Charlemagne, he invited scholars to his court, and established schools. He had those books that he considered 'most necessary for all men to know' translated from Latin into the native tongue. He himself learned Latin and translated the *Cura Pastoralis* (*Pastoral Rule*) of Pope Gregory the Great. He sponsored the creation of the *Anglo-Saxon Chronicle*, a history running back to Roman times, so that his people could know their history. He tried to establish justice, introducing a code of law, attempting to limit the prosecution of blood quarrels and introducing strict penalties for breaking an oath.

ALFRED AND KNIGHTHOOD

In Alfred's time during the late 9th century early forms of knighthood were beginning to take shape in mainland Europe with the emergence of a military elite of mounted warriors rewarded for fighting with the possession of land. In Anglo-Saxon England, the army consisted largely of thegns – warriors bound to their aristocratic lords who took responsibility for maintaining them. Alfred's reign saw the beginning of the theory that warriors were a self-contained group whose existence was essential for good government and a stable society. From the time of the Church Fathers in the 1st–5th centuries AD, it was normal for scholars to debate the right ordering of society and to propose a threefold division – such as clergy,

monks and laity; or nobility, freemen and slaves. As part of his campaign to improve education in his kingdom, King Alfred learned Latin and translated *On Consolation* by the 6th-century Roman philosopher Boethius. To the translation Alfred added the statement that good government required a land that has a good number of people containing (in Anglo-Saxon) *'geberdmen, fyrdmen and weorcmen'* (men who pray, men who fight and men who work). This theory would play an important part in the Church's later view of knights and in the code of chivalry.

ALFRED AS A CHIVALRIC WARRIOR

After the Battle of Edington in 878 Alfred showed considerable forbearance to the defeated Danish force. The Saxon victory came after a period of desperate guerrilla warfare and a great victorious charge across country – it might have been understandable for Alfred and his army to slaughter their enemies. Instead they behaved with restraint.

However, like Charlemagne's defeated Germanic enemies, the Vikings discovered that the price of their defeat was conversion to Christianity. Danish leader Guthrum was baptized with Alfred standing as his godfather and personally raising him from the baptismal waters. Afterwards Alfred recognized Guthrum as an adoptive son. This ability to exhibit generosity in victory, and to recognize the noble qualities of his defeated opponent,

was subsequently made the hallmark of a chivalric warrior fighting according to the code of chivalry.

In his lifetime, as well as after his death, Alfred's contemporaries celebrated him as a Christian warrior. His leading soldiers fought with swords that were decorated with the cross and his troops said prayers on the field of battle; as a contrast, monks recording his exploits always made a point of describing the Danes as pagans. The Welsh monk Asser, who wrote Alfred's biography in 893, called him 'ruler of all Christians in the island of Britain'.

▶ *This heroic statue of King Alfred stands in Winchester, southern England, the place of the king's burial after his death on 26 October 899. The facts of his life were quickly embroidered with legend.*

THE RISE OF THE NORMANS

THE EXPORTERS OF KNIGHTHOOD

The Normans who invaded England in 1066 were descendants of the Viking warrior chieftain Rollo, or Robert, who was granted land in western France in 911 by King Charles III the Simple of West Francia. Between 911 and 1066, Rollo's descendants established a feudal society in Normandy. In warfare they used heavy cavalry and built castles. Following the conquest they imposed feudalism in England, and their descendants later exported it to the Holy Land on the First Crusade from 1095 to 1099.

ARRIVAL OF THE NORTHMEN

Scholars disagree as to whether Duke Rollo was originally Norwegian or Danish. He took part in an unsuccessful Viking siege of Paris in 886 and afterwards established a settlement at the mouth of the river Seine. Charles the Simple established this area as a buffer state against further Viking attacks by granting the lands to Rollo. As well as agreeing to fend off further Viking incursions, Rollo paid feudal homage to King Charles III and accepted baptism as a Christian under the name Robert. The deal was sealed in the Treaty of St Claire-sur-Epte in 911 and Robert married Charles's daughter.

Robert and the settlers were originally known as Northmen or Norsemen, and subsequently as Normans. They quickly

▼ *Viking raiders arrive off the coast of France in the late 9th century. Their warband mentality fed into Norman and later chivalric culture.*

expanded their territory, moving west, and Robert gained middle Normandy (Bassin, Bayeux, L'Huernin and Le Mans) from the king in 924 and Robert's son and successor, William Longsword (Duke William I of Normandy), was granted the seaboard of the Avranchin (the area near Mont St Michel) and the Contentin (the north part of the peninsula) in 933.

DUKE RICHARD I OF NORMANDY

William Longsword was murdered in 942 and a power struggle ensued, but William's illegitimate son finally regained control of Normandy as Duke Richard I. Richard I was known as Richard Sans Peur ('the Fearless'), and in his long reign (942–96) the feudal system was begun in his lands. Normandy was a wealthy realm, with the city of Rouen established as a successful trading centre. Coins bearing the name of Duke Richard I have been found as far afield as Russia and Scotland.

EXPANDING MILITARY POWER

Richard I was succeeded by his illegitimate son Duke Richard II, known as 'the Good'. In his reign Normandy became a great military power: many of his feudal vassals were powerful counts, with large bodies of mounted warriors in their service. Normandy also became a player on the international stage. Duke Richard II established political links with English royalty through the marriage of his sister, Emma of Normandy, to King Aethelred in 1002. However, in the same period he also allowed Danish Vikings to use ports in Normandy as their bases for repeated raids on England.

In 1013 the Danes invaded England, and Emma's sons by King Aethelred, Edward (later Edward the Confessor) and Alfred Atheling, went to Normandy as exiles. Emma remained in England and after Aethelred's death in 1016 went on to marry England's Danish king, Canute.

KING WILLIAM'S FATHER

Richard II was succeeded by his son as Duke Richard III, but Richard III died after just a year in power, and his brother Robert became Duke Robert II of Normandy. Some sources suggest he murdered Richard and he is sometimes known as Robert le Diable ('the Devil') for this reason; he may be connected to the legendary Norman knight of that name, who in the 12th–14th-century tales was the devil's own son and lived a life of the greatest depravity before seeking forgiveness from the pope and saving Rome three times from Islamic attack.

After providing military support for King Henry I of France, Duke Robert II was rewarded with the territory of the Vexin, near Rouen. (Around this time historians generally begin to identify the lands of Francia Occidentalis or West Francia as France and those of Francia Orientalis or East Francia as Germany.) However, despite his nickname of 'the devil', Robert II was clearly also a religious man. He was a sponsor of reform for monasteries in Normandy along the lines

of the new practices promoted by the Abbey of Cluny, and made a pilgrimage to Jerusalem. It was on his return from this voyage that he died in Nicaea (modern Iznik, Turkey) in 1035.

DUKE WILLIAM OF NORMANDY

Robert II fathered an illegitimate son, William, by Herleva, daughter of a tanner or embalmer from Falaise. On his father's death William le Bâtard ('the Bastard') succeeded to the dukedom of Normandy at the age of just eight. He was raised in the household of his late father's steward, Osbern Herfasston, and appears to have had an education alongside several other martial youths in the Norman ways of war, including sword-fighting, the skills of mounted horsemanship and even castle-building – like that of later generations of knights-to-be, as first page and then as squire.

Duke William's biographer, William of Poitiers, described William in his youth as being masterful in the saddle, cutting the air with his sword, grasping his shining shield, and striking fear into his opponent with his fearsome use of the lance. He was knighted by King Henry I of France at the age of 15, in *c.*1042–43. Before he invaded

▲ The ability of Duke William's mounted warriors to launch a swift counter-attack made the difference between defeat and victory at the Battle of Hastings in 1066. This image of Norman cavalry preparing to charge is from the Bayeux Tapestry.

England in 1066, William had proved himself a forceful warrior and leader of men, with victories in Brittany, Maine and Ponthieu.

FEUDAL INVASION

The Norman invasion of England in 1066 could be termed a 'feudal war'. William's noble vassals were fighting for the promise of titles and land if the invasion was a success. At the crucial Battle of Hastings King Harold's army fought entirely on foot behind a wall of shields, while William's cavalry played an important part in the victory – hitting the Anglo-Saxons with a mounted charge after some had lost their discipline and broken out to pursue a feigned Norman retreat. From the very start of the occupation of England, the Normans raised castles to hold conquered territory and frighten the populace, and imposed their own feudal society in place of England's existing nobility.

▼ Duke William of Normandy, enthroned as King William I of England, makes a grant of lands to Alain de Brittany in return for the promise of feudal military service.

THE FIRST KNIGHTS
AN EXCLUSIVE FRATERNITY

In the decades after the Norman conquest, in the feudal societies of France, Germany and Norman England, we see the emergence of the first true knights – men who were made knights in a formal ceremony that admitted them to an elite group of warriors. Modern historians argue that soldiers fighting on horseback in the 9th and 10th centuries should be viewed as mounted warriors, rather than true knights. These mounted warriors were, as we have seen, bound to their lords in the developing feudal system, in which they provided military service in return for the right to land. However, an essential element of knighthood was absent: the idea of the making of a knight through the formal admission to a chivalric brotherhood.

Within this view, figures such as Charlemagne and Alfred the Great can be seen as remarkable warrior-kings, as precursors of chivalry, but not as knights; and likewise while mounted soldiers

▼ Feudal service was rewarded with grants of land, so more prominent knights were able to establish themselves on large estates.

riding in the heavy cavalry of Duke Richard II of Normandy, for example, had many qualities of knights, their comradeship as bonded vassals of their lord lacked this quality of a brotherhood following a chivalric code.

SOCIAL STATUS OF KNIGHTS

As both feudalism and knighthood developed, knights became established as one level in an enormously stratified social grouping that also included the barons on their great estates, and poorer mounted warriors who were not admitted to knighthood and provided military service as squires. The relative social status of those formally called 'knights' was constantly shifting as it was challenged from above and below.

EQUALITY AND EXCLUSIVENESS

In theory, according to the code of chivalry, the brotherhood of knights was an elite, but all within it were equal. This equality probably derived from that of the knights' predecessors among the freemen who fought side by side for the Frankish kings. In this tradition knighthood was a reward

▲ The Christian Church sanctioned violence when it was performed in Christ's service. This 12th-century illustration is entitled 'The faithful knight leaving to battle Satan'.

for the brave, and all brave knights were equal. Only a knight could make a knight – but knighthood could be conferred upon anyone who had proved himself worthy of the accolade.

Yet knights were also often a social elite. This was in large part because their feudal rewards for military service set them up as wealthy landowners, who were able to use their position to acquire more land and pass great territories down the generations. On a practical level, it was also because the cost of a knight's equipment excluded poorer warriors.

It became a matter of official policy to maintain the exclusiveness of the knightly fraternity and to exert control over who might confer knighthood. From the early 12th century, royal pronouncements excluded various groups from being knighted. Some of the earlier exclusions were designed to keep the peace by preventing any rowdy elements from becoming knights, and in particular to prevent nobles quickly raising a rebel force through a mass knighting ceremony. For example, a German decree of 1152 excluded peasants from being knights, and in 1140 Roger II, Norman king of Sicily,

▶ *In this manuscript illustration, also from the 12th century, the devils represent vices and heresies. Drawing his sword, the knight prepares to impose Christian law.*

forbade the knighting of men who were liable to disturb the peace. In 1186 Holy Roman Emperor Frederick I banned both the sons of peasants and the sons of priests from being knighted – the latter on the grounds that since priests officially could not marry, their sons were illegitimate.

INHERITED QUALITIES

Gradually the idea developed that the qualities needed to be a knight could only be transmitted through inheritance: only the descendants of knights could be knights. In 1235 the Cortes of Catalonia declared: 'We establish that no man can be knighted unless he is the son of a knight.' Sometimes the ability or right to raise to knighthood those not descended from knights was restricted to kings. For example, Holy Roman Emperor Frederick II declared in 1231: 'No man who is not of knightly descent shall be made a knight

except by our licence or permission.' The royal prerogative could be valuable (see box). These kinds of exclusions were not in force in England. Moreover, even in Germany and France knights were still sometimes 'made' by other knights on the field of battle as a reward for valour.

A LEISURED CLASS

The feudal system delivered knights a leisured life. When not on campaign, they lived in grand style in their castles and fortified manor houses, subsidised by the hard labour of the peasants who worked the land on the grand estates. Knights were free to hunt and hawk, to practise their military skills in tournaments and to develop their taste for literature and music – songs of knightly bravery. In these circumstances the literature and ethos of chivalry developed.

A COMPLEX BOND

In its mature form, from the late 11th century – when European knights rode out against the warriors of Islam in the First Crusade (1095–99) – knighthood was a complex bond, a combination of a badge of warrior honour, a social distinction, an ethical challenge and a religious calling. To be a knight was often a sign of

valorous achievement, while it could also be a title inherited by birth, giving right to certain lands. A knight also voluntarily adopted a code of honour, a duty of service, and was blessed by the Church as a defender of the Christian faith, or *miles Christi* ('soldier of Christ').

▼ *According to chivalric theory, the knight offered his military service to God. Knights and their swords were blessed in church.*

KNIGHTHOODS FOR SALE

Once it was accepted that generally men could not rise to knighthood from lower social ranks, except by royal licence, kings faced the temptation of raising money by putting knighthoods up for sale. This very unchivalric practice was particularly common in France, where for example the king, Philip IV (r. 1285–1314), announced his willingness to grant knighthoods for sums of money. In France in this era, a wealthy merchant might purchase a knighthood as a financial investment since being a knight brought exemptions from tax. Knighthoods were also sold by the Imperial crown in 14th-century Germany, by Charles IV, Holy Roman Emperor in 1355–78, and his subsequent successors.

CHAPTER TWO

BECOMING
A KNIGHT

The knight was a specialist in mounted fighting. He was well equipped, and often superbly well trained. Many knights underwent a long and difficult apprenticeship in the arts of war, and the thoroughness of this training set them apart from their contemporaries. Although some great martial figures were able to break into knighthood through acts of great chivalry, knights were generally a social elite of princes, magnates or the sons of knights.

In the 13th century the chivalric handbooks that provided instructions on proper knightly behaviour set guidelines on the kind of people who might properly aspire to knighthood. The most celebrated, the *Libre del Orde de Cavalleria* (*Book of the Order of Chivalry*), was written in *c*.1265 by the remarkable Majorcan troubadour, philosopher, novelist, mystic and missionary Ramon Llull. The book also teaches that it is essential for knights to come from a noble family because such families have an established tradition of chivalric virtue going back generations.

Another handbook, the *Livre de Chevalerie,* or *Book of Chivalry,* was written in *c*.1350 by French knight Geoffroi de Charny. He stresses the role of chivalric warriors in keeping the peace, and presents them as an arm of the Church alongside the priesthood. Chivalry (the class of knights and men at arms) supports the divinely sanctioned social structure, by making it possible for God's representatives on earth, the king and the Church authorities, to exercise authority and ensure that justice is done.

▲ *The late medieval Bodiam Castle, in East Sussex, England.*

◄ *By tradition, a squire was expected to keep vigil on the last night before he was elevated to the brotherhood of knights.*

ACQUIRING COURTESY

LIFE AS A PAGE

In theory the son of a knight was educated for knighthood from birth. Until the age of seven he was in the care of his mother and her women of the household, then he began the first stage of his knightly training as a page, either at home or in another noble house. Life as a page lasted for seven years before, at around the age of 14, a page moved on to complete his apprenticeship by serving a true knight day by day as his squire. In the later period of his life as a page he was sometimes known as a *damoiseau,* or valet.

▼ *The education of children was divided strictly by gender. While girls learned to spin, sew and manage the household, boys were instructed in martial arts, as shown in this 15th-century illustration.*

FIGHTING AND HUNTING

Squires of the household instructed the pages in horse-riding, tilting at the quintain (riding at and striking a target with a couched lance), tilting at the ring (striking a smaller round target), wrestling, boxing and running. The quintain was a human-shaped dummy holding a shield, and suspended on a stick: the page had to hit the shield right in the centre. The dummy would swing round and round and the page had to be careful to get swiftly out of the way.

The pages also learned how to handle a sword, practising their strokes against a 'pell', or wooden stake. They were trained in hunting techniques, such as caring for the hawks and falcons, and how to use a bow and arrow in competition

GEOFFREY CHAUCER

English poet Geoffrey Chaucer, whose portraits of a knight and a squire in *The Canterbury Tales* are celebrated for their authenticity, was a page at the court of Elizabeth de Burgh, countess of Ulster. The countess was married to Prince Lionel, duke of Clarence and second son of King Edward III of England, and Chaucer served as a squire in Lionel's company during the Hundred Years War in France. Captured while fighting at the siege of Rheims in 1360, Chaucer was ransomed for a handsome sum – the king himself contributed £16 to the fee. After these early military adventures, Chaucer spent most of his life as a courtier – like many young men who passed through the chivalric education system, he did not progress beyond being a squire and was never knighted. Chaucer was clearly an extraordinarily gifted and talented man, and it is apparent from his later work, which shows that he could read Latin and French, that the quality of education available to all pages and squires in the royal and noble households of this period was of a very high standard – in book learning as well as in chivalric accomplishments.

les 2 enfans de octouier

with their peers. They learned how to handle animal carcasses and prepare them for the kitchen – for example how to cut up a deer.

By watching and helping the squire, the pages also learned to perform the duties that would be required of them when they were older, whether serving knights in hall, working in the kennels and hawkpens, tending horses in the stable or cleaning and storing helmets, armour and weapons in the armoury. They learned

▶ *Pages were trained to serve alongside squires and kitchen staff during banquets. The guest of honour at this feast is Edward the Confessor.*

how to wait at table and carve meat and how to clean armour, weapons and chain mail by rubbing it in a barrel of sand.

In addition the squires were responsible for the pages' training in the courtly arts of singing, dancing, playing the pipes and the harp, and learning Latin and French. These skills were important accomplishments for a mature knight, so it was vital that this area of a page's education was not neglected. The actual teaching of writing and singing was entrusted to minor clergy and to travelling troubadours. The visiting priest would also give the pages religious education.

CORRECTION

If pages were unwilling to learn any part of their studies, squires were permitted to 'correct' them with physical force. No doubt squires were able to get away with a good deal under cover of 'corrections' and probably made themselves feel better

▼ *As well as teaching the pages to read and write, priests made sure that the young men had a proper grounding in Christianity.*

about their own mistreatment when they were pages by handing out orders and harsh punishments.

The pages had a gentler time with the ladies of the household, who also took an interest in the young men's education in chivalric arts, helping with writing and teaching dancing, courtly manners and gallant behaviour. They taught the pages necessary skills of hygiene and personal grooming. The ladies also played chess and other games with them.

BOARDING SCHOOL FOR PAGES

It was normal practice for a son to be sent to the house of his father's *suzerain* (his superior within the feudal system) to undergo his chivalric education in the company of the children of other knights. A lord's son was generally sent to the castle of another great lord or bishop – for example, Stephen of Blois (the future King Stephen of England, and the son of Stephen of Blois who was one of the leaders of the First Crusade) was sent to the court of his uncle, King Henry I of England, at about the age of ten, in 1106. Prominent churchmen took princes and the sons of noble houses into their establishments, to instruct them in the ways of chivalry. Thomas Becket received Henry II's son Henry (later 'the Young King')

alongside princes and nobles of neighbouring kingdoms. He oversaw their education until they attained knighthood.

Above all, pages learned 'courtesy', meaning the kind of behaviour that could only be picked up at a lordly or princely court. The Latin word *curialitas* can be translated as 'courtesy' or 'courtliness', the behaviour practised at the *curia*, or court.

▼ *Pages were expected to learn how to feed, groom and soothe horses belonging to the squires and the knight they served.*

AT A KNIGHT'S RIGHT HAND

LIFE AS A SQUIRE

The second stage of a chivalric education, after seven years living as a page, was often seven or more years' senior service to a knight as a squire. Typically, this began at around the age of 14. In these cases, squires cared for their lords, the knights whom they served, in all things. They attended to the knights' needs in the castle or manor house, at chivalric tournaments and on the field of battle.

It is important to note, however, that not all squires were trainee knights. There were many mounted warriors who, having progressed from being a page to becoming a squire, remained squires into mature adulthood, and even for their whole lives, because they were never formally dubbed into knighthood. Many had all the skill, bravery and chivalric

▼ *As well as serving wine and food at mealtimes, one of a squire's duties in the banqueting hall was to bring water for guests to wash their hands.*

accomplishments of their knightly counterparts. At the same time, many more junior squires served in the knightly household and oversaw the education of pages as described on the previous section and below.

▲ *Life as a knight or a squire required a fit, strong body. Practice was needed to develop the skills with sword and lance.*

AT HOME

When a squire was young, and still learning the arts of chivalry in the service of his lord, he generally lived in the castle alongside his fellows, usually sharing sleeping quarters. The young men took turns to serve the lord and other knights. In the hall the squires carved meat, and served food and wine at banquets. They also worked in the knight's bedchamber, making the bed, helping the knight dress and bringing a *vin de coucher* (draught of wine before sleep). It was also one of the squire's duties to sleep in the knight's chamber or at his door if requested. Squires worked with the animals in the kennels and stables and looked after the armoury. They also taught the pages in the house.

Squires also served the ladies of the castle. They were permitted to mingle with them quite freely, playing chess, walking in the garden, going hunting and hawking in their company. It was quite common for scandals to arise when these interactions became too intimate.

▲ *Three knights are dressed and armed by their squires, prior to a knighting ceremony.*

AT TOURNAMENTS AND ON CAMPAIGN

If the knight travelled to a tournament, the squire accompanied him. The squire fought in the mêlée, the mock battle that was held at the start of some tournaments. For jousting he had to prepare the knight's horses and be on hand to provide fresh lances and equipment. The squires gathered behind the barriers at the edge of the lists or tournament competition area, ready to rush to the knight's assistance if needed.

When the knight went on military campaign, two squires served him together. They fought alongside him, and were responsible for ensuring he had a good supply of weapons and fresh horses.

Another key part of the squire's training was learning and practising the arts of fighting, jousting and horse-riding. Squires began by fighting without chain mail or other armour in order to accustom themselves to handling the great lances and heavy swords that were used at tournaments and in battle. For example, they would practise hitting targets with their lances while running. Then they would move on to practising with the weapons while wearing armour. The young men needed to be fit and strong to cope with chain mail, for example, because it could weigh as much as 22.5kg (50lb) and the

suit's entire weight was felt on the shoulders. Finally they would be ready to practise fighting and jousting while on horseback.

The squires were also educated in other aspects of courtly life and chivalry such as hunting, hawking, dancing and the appreciation of poetry and music. Some learned to read. They were introduced to historical chronicles, books on hunting and battlefield chivalry and treatises on how to be a knight such as Ramon Llull's *Book of the Order of Chivalry*, as well as chivalric romances and songs of courtly love. Squires also learned the basics of blazonry – the language of heraldry, the science of recognizing and interpreting coats of arms. Squires were also responsible for overseeing the education of pages in all these aspects of chivalric life.

LIFELONG SERVICE AS A SQUIRE

As mentioned earlier, not all squires progressed to become knights. Some seem to have fought in campaign after campaign alongside knights and remained squires. Some came from families that could not afford the expense of the ceremony and the equipment needed to be a knight. There were certainly plenty of opportunities for men of this class, well educated in the ways of chivalry, to serve at royal and noble courts throughout Europe whether as warrior squires, heralds or – if they had literary talent – as poets or chroniclers. Examples of notable men of letters who did not progress beyond being squires are Geoffrey Chaucer, author of *The Canterbury Tales*, and Ramon Llull, author of the *Book of the Order of Chivalry*.

KNIGHTING

The ceremony of knighting marked the end of the chivalric apprenticeship as page and then squire. Squires who were princes or the sons of great lords could look forward to being knighted in a great courtly ceremony. A prince would often be knighted with a host of his fellow squires to make the ceremony more magnificent. In 1306, for example, Edward of Caernarfon (the future King Edward II of

England) was knighted in a ceremony involving 276 squires. He followed the prescribed rituals for preparing to be knighted, including keeping vigil overnight, then was knighted by his father before he himself knighted all the other participants. The main ceremony was held in the grounds of the London Temple, and tents were raised there to accommodate the great crowd of squires. Even so, the space was so full that two knights died in the crush, several others collapsed in a faint, and there was even a fight. There were many other similar examples – such as that of Ulrich von Lichtenstein, knight and poet, who was one of 250 squires raised to knighthood when Duke Leopold of Austria celebrated the wedding of his daughter in 1222.

Some squires of a modest background but with great martial ability were able to win knighthood on the basis of their deeds – for it was possible to be knighted on the field of battle after achieving a great feat or prior to the beginning of fighting.

▼ *Squires attended to a knight's needs in the heat of battle and on campaign, helping him with his weapons and armour.*

ARISE, SIR KNIGHT
THE ORIGINS AND DEVELOPMENT OF THE KNIGHTING CEREMONY

The central event in a knight's life was the occasion on which he was knighted. In this proud moment, he was admitted to an elite international group, a brotherhood of equals bound by the demanding code of chivalry. He dedicated himself to serving God, the Church, his king and his lord.

The ceremonies of knighting developed from ceremonial rites of passage practised in ancient Rome and among Germanic tribes in the Roman Empire. In Rome, when a boy was of age to become a man he was given the *toga virilis*, a white toga worn by citizens of the empire. Among Germanic tribes of the 1st and 2nd centuries AD, according to the Roman historian Tacitus, when a young man was ready to assume adult status he was given a sword and shield in a public ceremony by his father, a relative or the tribal chief. Afterwards he was counted among the tribe's warriors.

▼ *According to some accounts, it was in the Norman tradition that only knights could make others knights, and the Anglo-Saxon tradition was to be knighted by a priest.*

INVESTED WITH A SWORD
In the 8th and 9th centuries, a similar coming-of-age ceremony was used among the Germanic tribes for their princes and young lords: the young man was presented with a sword or a sword-belt. Charlemagne's son Louis the Pious, for example, was ceremonially invested with his sword in 791 at Regensburg, in preparation for going on a military campaign with his great father against the Avars. By the late 10th and early 11th centuries, in France and Norman England, the ceremony was being used to describe the elevation of a footsoldier into a mounted warrior; in the ceremony the footsoldier was given the equipment he would need to serve as a knight.

This was originally a secular event, but it became imbued with religious significance as the Christian Church developed doctrines that sanctified violence if performed in the defence of the Church and of God, and knights began to be seen as 'soldiers of Christ'. In Mainz, as early as the mid-10th century, the blessing of a sword and creation of a knight was incorporated into the Christian Mass: the sword was laid on the altar before the reading of the Holy Gospel and this prayer was read: 'Hearken, we pray, O Lord, to our intercessions, and bless with the right hand of thy greatness this sword, with which thy Servant wishes to be girded, that it may be used to defend churches, widows and orphaned children, and all thy people against the attacks of pagans, and that it may strike terror into doers of evil and may be used in justice both to attack and to defend.' Attendants then girded the sword on the aspirant knight.

DUBBING A KNIGHT
Elaborate protocol grew up around the knighting ceremony. The experience of being knighted could be very different depending on the circumstances or the

▲ *After a squire was knighted it was a matter of honour for him to seek an opportunity to prove himself worthy of his knighthood.*

custom prevailing at various times in the chivalric period. For some princely or lordly warriors, knighting took place in the courtly and religious ceremony of investiture, in the presence of a bishop and often at the hand of a king, among many noble peers. For others it was a simpler, though still religiously charged event involving confession and attendance at Mass, while for some squires, knighting was performed on the battlefield – in the simple act of dubbing – either before fighting began or else during or after the battle as a reward for an act of valour.

Dubbing consisted of striking the aspirant knight a blow either with the hand or a sword. In French the blow was known as the *collée* or *paumée* – later it was known in English as an 'accolade'. The striking of the blow may have derived from the ancient Roman practice of slapping a slave to set him or her free, or else from a Germanic tradition of hitting the witnesses to a legal agreement (presumably this was to ensure that they did not forget what they had seen).

THE MEANING OF DUBBING

From at least the 11th century in England and France, dubbing was an important part of knighting ceremonies, both at court and on campaign – the earliest known use of the verb 'to dub' comes in the *Anglo-Saxon Chronicle* for 1086, which records that at Whitsuntide that year King William I 'dubbed his son Henry in making him a knight'. Until the mid-14th century dubbing was found only in England and France, but subsequently it became accepted as one of the essential parts of any knighting ceremony, whether simple or grand.

There is considerable debate among historians about the meaning of the dubbing ceremony. In addition to admitting warriors to the chivalric elite and providing them with the status and equipment that would enable them to function as a knight, the ceremony often also marked the delegation from a lord to the new knight of legal authority to perform

▶ *One of the parallels of the chivalric knighting ceremony was the practice in the 10th century of 'making a knight' by presenting him with military equipment needed to fight in battles and tournaments.*

▲ *Armed soldiers look on as Charlemagne invests a young man as a member of his warrior band. Earlier rituals like this lay behind the development of the formal knighting ceremonies of the Middle Ages.*

feudal duties in his name. In the 11th century the class of knights was increasingly presented as a body created by God to keep order, as a secular arm of His Church. From around this time, bishops were present at formal knighting ceremonies. However, the involvement of

▲ *By the late 15th century, the investiture of knights had developed from the days of Charlemagne into a much more complex ritual, with specific stages that all had distinct religious overtones.*

ordained clergy, and the development of a religious rationale for knightly warfare, did not alter one key element of knighting: only a knight could make a knight. Entrance to the chivalric brotherhood could only be conferred by one who was already a member.

BE THOU A KNIGHT!

ACHIEVING KNIGHTHOOD

Accounts in chronicles and romances make it clear that the simplest form of knighting, performed on the battlefield in the immediate aftermath of some great military feat, with the blood still wet on the weapons, was the most highly prized of all. It was probably a very simple ceremony – perhaps no more than a *collée* or blow accompanied by the words 'Be thou a knight'.

If it were possible to achieve this, undergoing such a battlefield ceremony before the fighting began was a very good option for a squire of modest means. Not only did it avoid the need for a costly courtly ceremony, but it also greatly improved the squire's prospects in battle:

a knight could earn more per day than a squire, and was also far less likely to be killed if he were captured in the fighting – for his status as a knight would ensure that he was treated with great respect and ransomed.

KNIGHTED AFTER AN ACT OF GREAT BRAVERY

The great Breton warrior Bertrand du Guesclin, who was a French commander during the Hundred Years War between France and England, was a member of the select band of warriors to be knighted on the battlefield.

Serving Marshal Arnoul d'Audrehem, the French king's lieutenant in Normandy,

du Guesclin was honoured at Easter in 1354 after he defeated a raid led by the English knight Sir Hugh Calverley. Du Guesclin and the Marshal were on reconnaissance in Brittany and staying in the castle of Montmauron, 6 miles (10km) from the key English stronghold of Bécherel, which was commanded by Sir Hugh. Guessing that Sir Hugh might launch an assault on the castle in a bid to capture Marshal d'Audrehem, du Guesclin

▼ *According to chronicler Jean Froissart, at the Battle of Aljubarrota in 1385 between Portugal and Castile, 140 Castilians and 60 Portuguese were knighted. The Portuguese knights, fighting in the front rank, prevailed.*

hid a group of archers beside the route from Bécherel to Montmauron. When the attack came, du Guesclin heard his archers fighting the English and rode out with Marshal d'Audrehem to take part in the battle. In the course of the conflict, Sir Hugh Calverley was flung to the ground and taken prisoner, and afterwards du Guesclin was knighted on the field of battle by Eslatre des Mares, Captain of Caen Castle.

KNIGHTED BEFORE BATTLE

Many squires were knighted at the start of a campaign or before battle commenced. This was partly done for practical reasons – tradition demanded that a squire be knighted before he could command troops in battle.

Sometimes squires were knighted in a great hurry as a battle was about to start. According to historian Jean Froissart (c.1337–1410) in his *Chronicles*, several knights were made in this way in the English army at Vironfosse in 1338. The French and English forces were arrayed in the field, and the morning passed without battle being joined, but at around noon a hare broke from cover in the front part of the French army and ran hither and thither, causing the soldiers there to shout and laugh; this noise was interpreted in the rear part of the English army as the sound of the first fighting of the day, and

▼ *Breton knight Bertrand du Guesclin kneels before King Charles V. He was raised from humble origins by his bravery and skill.*

several squires were knighted there and then in order to take part in the battle as knights. The Earl of Hainault made 14 knights in this way; afterwards when it was revealed what had happened these men became known as the 'Knights of the Hare'.

Sir James Douglas, the Scottish knight named the 'Black Douglas' by the English for his fierce border raiding, was another great warrior dubbed on the battlefield – in his case, prior to battle, on 24 June 1314 at Bannockburn.

THE BLACK PRINCE AT CRÉCY

Another knight who swiftly proved his worth as a chivalric warrior was Edward Prince of Wales (later known as 'the Black Prince'), the 16-year-old son of King Edward III of England. The king knighted the prince along with several of the young man's peers at the start of the French campaign of 1346; then on 26 August, at the Battle of Crécy, he placed his young son in charge of the right wing of his army, with Sir Godfrey Harcourt to assist him, and he himself stood back watching the engagement from a windmill nearby.

▲ *This 15th-century illustration of the Battle of Crécy from an edition of Froissart's* Chronicles *gives the foreground to English longbowmen. The battle was a famous victory for the English and for Edward, the Black Prince.*

According to the account in Froissart's *Chronicles*, the fighting was very hard on the Black Prince's wing of the army, and Sir Godfrey Harcourt called for reinforcements, but Edward III refused, saying 'let the boy win his spurs'. By this Edward (or more likely Froissart, who put the words in his mouth) meant that the prince should prove himself worthy of the gilded spurs that were a mark of knighthood.

He did so. The prince fought on and the English prevailed in the battle. When fighting at Crécy finished, after dark, the French had lost no fewer than 1,542 knights. The battle was remembered as significant in two ways – a humiliating disaster for France and a great triumph for the English army – and proof beyond doubt that Prince Edward had a great future ahead of him as a knight.

THE MEANING OF KNIGHTING
THE RELIGIOUS SYMBOLISM OF THE KNIGHTING CEREMONY

In his *Book of Chivalry* (c.1350) Geoffroi de Charny gives an idealized account of the knighting ceremony. His version is based on that given a little over a century earlier in an anonymous French poem called *L'Ordre de Chevalerie* (c.1225), and presents an account of what should, or ideally might, happen rather than what did routinely occur. The kind of ceremony he describes is rich in religious symbolism. De Charny also provides detailed explanations of the significance of the various parts of the ritual.

RETREAT AND PREPARATION

According to de Charny, a squire was expected to prepare himself to join the blessed company of knights by confessing his sins and receiving communion. On the day before the ceremony, the squire was to take a bath, then rest in a bed newly made with perfectly white sheets. At the given hour, knights were to come to the squire's bedroom to dress him in new white linen, scarlet robes and black stockings, with a white girdle and a scarlet cloak. They would lead him in the evening to church, where he would spend the night in lonely vigil.

In the morning the knights would accompany him to Mass, at which he should pray for divine grace to make him fit to serve as a knight. After Mass, the knights would lead the squire into the presence of the knight who was to confer the order of knighthood upon him. This knight would attach a gilded spur to the squire's foot, gird the squire with a sword and kiss him to confirm the conferral of knighthood. Finally the knight would dub the squire, delivering the accolade or *collée* on his shoulder.

The *Book of Chivalry* explains the knighting ceremony as follows. When the squire takes a bath on the day before he is to be knighted, he washes away the accumulated sins of a lifetime and emerges with a clean conscience. Then when he rests in a bed newly made with white sheets, this symbolizes the deep sense of peace that arises when his conscience is clean, and he has won God's forgiveness for past wrongdoing. When he is dressed in new white clothes these symbolize his new virtue, while the scarlet robes signify the blood he must be willing to spill in defending Christianity and the Church. The black stockings stand for the earth from which the squire came and to which he will return, and the fact that since he cannot know the hour of his own death he should turn away resolutely from pride and vainglory. His white girdle signifies chastity, and his scarlet cloak is a traditional sign of humility.

Then he keeps a vigil through the night, and this symbolizes that he must be

▼ *King Edward III of England, enthroned, looks on as Edward the Black Prince is invested as a knight of the Most Noble Order of the Garter in 1348. Members wore the garter on their armour in battle or in tournaments as a badge of honour.*

always watchful and renounce evil. When he is given a golden spur in the moment of knighting, this signifies that he must never be covetous, for gold is the most precious and widely coveted of metals but the knight wears it on his foot rather than on his head or close to his heart. When he is girded with a sword, this signifies that he must support justice and reason, defending both the Christian faith and the Church, and when the knight kisses him it is a sign of peace, loyalty and love. The accolade or blow on the shoulder signifies that he should not forget that he is now a knight and must behave henceforth in accordance with the laws of chivalry.

CHIVALRIC SYMBOLISM IN *THE ORDER OF CHIVALRY*

The anonymous French poem, *L'Ordre de Chevalerie*, that provided de Charny with the basis of his inspirational account, describes a fictional encounter between a Christian knight and the great Kurdish Muslim warrior and general Saladin, who captured Jerusalem in 1187 and fought against King Richard I of England during the Third Crusade (1189–1192). The Christian knight, Hue de Tabarie, is captured by Saladin, who was renowned for his chivalric behaviour but, as a non-Christian, could not be expected to know the ceremonies of knighthood. Saladin offers to set Hue free if he will instruct him in the meanings of knighthood and then make him a knight. Hue is not keen to agree this bargain, for he knows that Saladin cannot truly become a knight because he does not accept the Christian faith, but as a prisoner he has little choice.

Hue de Tabarie cuts Saladin's hair and beard, then leads the way to a bath that signifies – as it did for the knight in the *Book of Chivalry* – the washing away of sins, here specifically identified with the Christian rite of baptism. Afterwards Hue takes Saladin to a magnificent bed, which

▶ *Saladin, the crusaders' greatest Muslim foe, exhibited such magnanimity and chivalry in victory that he was hailed as a 'Saracen knight'. He is said to have been knighted in 1167 by Humphrey III of Toron, Constable of the Kingdom of Jerusalem.*

is said to symbolize the place in Paradise that each true knight will attain, then dresses him in white and a scarlet robe, again signifying the willingness to shed blood in chivalric encounters. He then girds on the sword but stops short of giving Saladin the accolade on the grounds that he cannot administer this because he is Saladin's prisoner.

THE SYMBOLISM OF KNIGHTLY FIGHTING EQUIPMENT

Knighting rituals developed from simpler ceremonies in which young men were given the equipment they needed to be warriors or mounted knights. In the literature of chivalry, symbolism was attached not only to the elements of the knighting ceremony but also to the fighting equipment a knight used. In the French prose romance *Lancelot* (*c*.1225), also known as the *Prose Lancelot*, the Arthurian knight Sir Lancelot is instructed in the symbolism of his armour by the Lady of the Lake. She tells him that his armour signifies various aspects of the duty that he and every Christian knight owes to the Church. His hauberk, or mail tunic, protects his body just as he should defend the Church; his helmet covers his head and symbolizes the way in which he should guard the Church; as his great lance, expertly wielded, strikes fear into wicked men, so it stands for his power to keep the enemies of the Church at bay. His mighty sword has two edges, which stand for the fact that he serves both God and the people, and a sharp point, which signifies that the people must be obedient and follow his leadership. The horse on which he rides stands for the people of the Christian world who support him and follow his guidance, just as a horse follows the directions of its rider.

▼ *King Francis I of France considered it a great honour when he was dubbed a knight by French chivalric hero Pierre du Terrail, the Chevalier de Bayard. This romanticized depiction suggests that the event was blessed by a shaft of light falling from heaven.*

HOTSPUR

SIR HENRY PERCY

Sir Henry Percy was probably the greatest knight of the late 14th century, whose effectiveness in patrolling England's border with Scotland – and especially his speed of movement and willingness to attack – won him the nickname 'Hotspur' from his Scottish foes. He was a valued servant and trusted military leader for the English kings Richard II and Henry IV, although he eventually rebelled against both. He was renowned for his knightly prowess, both in the lists and on the field of battle. The chronicler Jean Froissart declared that Hotspur 'desired feats of arms above all other things, and was always first into action at the barriers'.

A PRODIGIOUS YOUTH

Hotspur was raised to arms. He was born at Alnwick Castle, Northumberland, in 1364, the son of another Henry Percy, 1st Earl of Northumberland, and the earl's

▼ *Hotspur was England's hero at the Battle of Otterburn in 1388. This two-panelled illustration is to a line from the poet Robert Burns's celebration of the battle, 'But Persie wi his gude braid sword'.*

SIR HENRY PERCY
Born: 20 May 1364
Died: 21 July 1403
Knighted: 1377
Famous for: raiding victories against Scots on England's northern border
Greatest achievement: victory in Battle of Homildon Hill, 1402

wife Margaret, who was of the proud Neville family of Raby. Contrary to normal practice, Hotspur was knighted at the age of just 13 in 1377 by King Edward III. The following year, aged 14, he fought alongside his father in retaking Berwick Castle from Scottish raiders.

In 1379 Hotspur married Elizabeth Mortimer, daughter of Edmund Mortimer, 3rd Earl of March, and in 1380 he campaigned with his father-in-law in Ireland. In 1383 Hotspur went on crusade in Prussia against pagan Lithuanians – at this time, the military order of the Teutonic Knights organized crusading trips in Prussia and the Baltic region for the nobility of Europe.

SCOURGE OF THE SCOTS

In 1385 King Richard II of England appointed Hotspur the Warden of the East March (border region) of Scotland, charged with controlling Scottish raiders in the region. In the same year Hotspur accompanied the king's army into Scotland. In 1386 Richard sent him to the aid of the English garrison in Calais, France, because an attack was expected from the French; while there, Hotspur led a number of raids in Picardy.

In 1388 Hotspur was nominated as a Knight of the Garter and returned to the Scottish border. That year he rode into Scotland and fought James Douglas, 2nd Earl of Douglas, at the Battle of Otterburn, which was partly fought in moonlight, and was celebrated by Froissart for being 'as hard a meeting, as well-fought a struggle as ever was'. In this heroic clash, Douglas was killed but Hotspur was captured and ransomed by the Scots. The greater part of his substantial ransom – 7,000 marks – was paid from royal funds and by a subscription from Parliament.

Hotspur's reputation as a knight continued to grow. He took on his fellows in chivalric tournaments, and won admiration for his performance in the lists, notably in the Jousts of St Inglevert that were held near Calais in 1390, and at Smithfield, London, during the celebration of Richard II's 1396 marriage to Isabella of France. He was entrusted by the king with diplomatic missions to Cyprus, to the duchy of Aquitaine and to Calais in 1394–96, and in 1396 was once again appointed Warden of the East March, this time for a period of ten years.

REBEL KNIGHT

Yet despite so much evidence of royal favour, Hotspur turned against Richard II and sided with his opponent Henry Bolingbroke. Hotspur and his father may

▶ *Alnwick Castle, Hotspur's birthplace, was built in the late 11th century to guard England's northern border against the Scots. The Percy family bought it in 1309 and it remains in the family's hands to this day.*

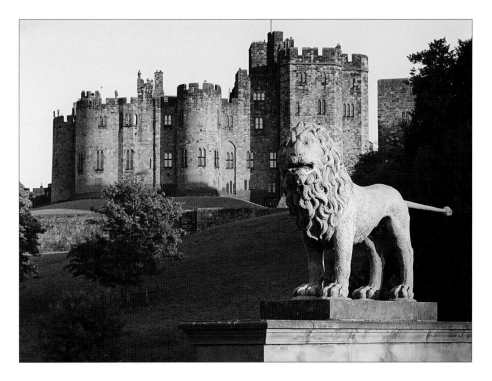

have felt that Richard was undermining their authority in the border region, for he took the town of Berwick out of their control; they may have believed that the king was acting in tyrannical fashion in his campaign against the Duke of Gloucester, his nephew Henry Bolingbroke and the earls of Arundel and Warwick. When in 1399 Bolingbroke returned from the exile into which Richard had cast him in an attempt to seize the throne, Hotspur threw his lot in with Henry, meeting him at Doncaster and riding south in his support.

Once established as King Henry IV, Bolingbroke rewarded Hotspur handsomely. He made him Sheriff of Northumberland, Lord of Bamburgh and Justiciar of North Wales and Chester, as well as giving him a further appointment

▼ *Hotspur had undoubted greatness as a military commander and as a knight in the saddle. But he displayed little loyalty, twice rebelling against his king – Richard II in 1399 and Henry IV in 1403. This is his effigy, at Wells Cathedral, Somerset.*

as Warden of the East March. The appointment in Wales brought him control of the great castles of Beaumaris, Caernarfon, Chester, Conway and Flint. In 1401 Hotspur again proved his prowess by capturing Conway Castle, which had fallen to Welsh rebels, and in the next year trounced the Scots at the Battle of Homildon Hill, capturing several lords including Archibald, Earl of Douglas.

KILLED AT SHREWSBURY

In the wake of this success he rebelled against Henry IV, accusing him of tyrannical government and the breaking of oaths. Hotspur was angry at various royal decisions that he perceived as slights, including Henry's establishment of a military command in Wales under Henry, Prince of Wales. Open conflict ensued. Hotspur led an army south to fight forces under the command of the Prince of Wales at Shrewsbury, but on arriving was surprised to discover a larger royal army led by King Henry IV himself. In the battle that followed, Hotspur was killed – reputedly when he raised the visor of his helmet to gulp some air and was shot in the mouth by an arrow. On seeing the death of their proud leader, the Percy forces abandoned the fight.

Despite the rebellion, King Henry wept when he saw the corpse of his former friend. He ordered Hotspur's burial at Whitchurch in Shropshire, but then had him disinterred. Henry wanted to display the body to counter rumours that Hotspur was still alive and also to make an example of him as a rebel against royal authority. He put Hotspur's corpse on display in Shrewsbury marketplace supported by a pair of millstones, and afterwards had his body cut into four and sent to the four corners of the kingdom. The former knight's head was displayed on a pole at the gates of York.

SHAKESPEARE'S HOTSPUR

Hotspur's fame among later generations rests in part on his appearance as a character in William Shakespeare's historical play *King Henry IV Part I*. Shakespeare rewrites history by making the knight the same age as Prince Henry ('Hal') whereas in reality Hotspur was a good deal older than the future king. The play contrasts Prince Hal's seeming indolence as a young man with Hotspur's great energy, force and bravery.

HOW TO BE A KNIGHT
MANUALS OF CHIVALRY

In the 14th and 15th centuries chivalric manuals such as Ramon Llull's *Book of the Order of Chivalry* were read at courts across Europe. Written in Majorca in the Catalan language in *c*.1265, Llull's book was widely translated and editions have survived that were published in France, Scotland and London – the last a translation by English printer William Caxton, printed in 1484, the year after he published the second edition of Geoffrey Chaucer's *The Canterbury Tales* and the year before he published Sir Thomas Malory's *Le Morte d'Arthur*.

The *Book of the Order of Chivalry* describes an encounter between a hermit and a squire at the former's forest hermitage. The hermit was once a great and wise knight, who had enjoyed a long and glorious chivalric career, in the course of which he had won many renowned victories in battle and excelled at tournaments held for the pleasure of kings and

RAMON LLULL

Ramon Llull, author of the *Book of the Order of Chivalry*, was a remarkable man with many very powerful talents. He is celebrated as a philosopher and religious mystic, as a poet and the author in 1284 of the allegorical novel *Blanquerna*, the first major work of literature in the Catalan language. But perhaps above all he is remembered as the developer of a means of marshalling information by combining attributes from lists: he developed the method, which he published in the *Ars inveniendi veritatis* ('Art of Finding Truth') and the *Ars Magna* ('Great Art'), as a way to reduce doctrine to first principles for use in attempts to convert Muslims to Christianity. His method – claimed by some as an antecedent of modern information science – is commonly known by the name *ars combinatoria*, applied to it by the 17th-century German philosopher Gottfried Liebniz.

Born in Ciutat de Majorca (probably Palma) in Majorca in *c*.1232, Llull had a chivalric education as page and squire at the royal court of Majorca. He married, then at the age of about 30 (just before he wrote his chivalric manual) he had five visions of Christ crucified, that inspired him to become a lay Franciscan and later a missionary to Muslims in northern Africa and Asia Minor. He visited North Africa three times on mission, on one occasion carrying out reconnaissance for a possible crusade, and according to legend was stoned by angry Muslims at Bejaïa (Bougie) – or perhaps at Tunis – and died in 1315 a Christian martyr on the voyage home.

▲ *Like the hermit knight in the* Book of the Order of Chivalry, *Arthurian knight Sir Lancelot spent a large part of his life in rural retreat. Lancelot was cared for and educated by the Lady of the Lake.*

princes and their ladies. He had often risked his life for the glory of knighthood and in all his dealings had shown wisdom and nobility of character as well as courage and physical strength. Nearing the end of his career, he was aware that his physical strength was failing and rather than attempt to perform acts of chivalry at a level below his customary excellence, he had chosen to retire to a hermitage. A young squire, meanwhile, was riding through the forest on his way to the king's winter court nearby, but he failed to keep his wits about him and fell asleep in the saddle; his horse wandered off the path into the depths of the forest and came to the hermitage.

DEFENDERS OF HONOUR

When the two met, and explained their positions, the hermit offered to teach the young squire all he could need to know about chivalry. He gave the squire a copy of a book on the subject, which contained all his wisdom.

The book explains that long ago, knights were picked from the general population, one from every thousand men, as defenders of justice; and the horse was placed at the service of the knight because of its beauty, speed and strength. It says that knights were an order set apart, coming in the natural social hierarchy above the people, and below the prince, whom the knights must serve alongside God. The knight's principal duties were to defend the honour of the prince and of the Church, and to uphold justice. It is right, the book says, for knights to strike fear into the hearts of the ordinary people, because this prevents the populace doing wrong. In the same way, as knights are placed in an elevated position of trust, it is therefore far worse when a knight does evil than when an ordinary peasant or farmer is wicked.

▼ *Chivalric manuals described how a knight should behave towards the poor, who might need charity as well as protection.*

▲ *Knights were expected to be skilled in the arts of hawking and hunting. Here a hunting party sets out from a castle.*

KNIGHTLY SKILLS

Knights must be taught and must practise essential chivalric skills such as horse-riding, jousting, sword fighting, and the hunting of lions, bears, stags and rabbits. These activities are important for a knight because they keep him fit for fulfilling his duties of chivalric service. A knight who despises the practice of knightly skills is one who despises the very institution of knighthood.

LARGESSE AND COURTESY

Other notable guides to chivalric behaviour include Geoffroi de Charny's *Book of Chivalry*, and an anonymous early 13th-century poem *Roman des Eles*. The *Roman des Eles* argues that chivalric courtesy derives from God and is possessed by knights. The poem has two key aspects: largesse and courtesy. All knights should be able to demonstrate largesse, it states; they should give freely, with boldness and even carelessness. Knights should demonstrate their courtesy by never displaying boastful behaviour, envy, slanderous talk and greed. Rather, they should take pleasure in music and songs, and always honour the Church.

De Charny addresses much of his teaching to men-at-arms, a group of chivalric warriors distinct from knights, from which he himself had emerged. He went on to become one of France's most prominent knights in the service of King John II. He was a member of the Order of the Star and was granted the honour of bearing the Oriflamme, the French standard, into battle. In his *Book of Chivalry* he argues that chivalric warriors should spend their lives striving; even the greatest of them should be seeking to achieve remarkable deeds that would bring them more honour still. He also argues that they can be driven to greater deeds by the fire of courtly love: they should love their lady for love's sake and achieve greatness in the quest for her love.

CHAPTER THREE

THE KNIGHT AT HOME

When a knight was not at war, he lived in his castle. If he were a substantial lord he kept his own castle, and if he were less well established he served with honour in the castle of his feudal superior. During peacetime he enjoyed strenuous pastimes such as hunting and tourneying (fighting in tournaments), which helped keep him ready for battle. The knightly class to which he belonged was supported by the labour of the peasants who farmed the lands of the fief, or feudal landholding, and whose agricultural produce supplemented the meat the knights caught in hunting. The knight therefore had plenty of leisure time in which to feast and enjoy the chivalric songs of travelling poets. He also had peacetime responsibilities and duties to carry out.

The knight's role in peacetime changed as feudalism developed. In the early years, he was a mounted soldier and little more, and in periods of peace his main job was to ride out in service of his feudal lord if the need arose, to protect the lord's interests or impose his authority. The knight had a duty to administer and govern his feudal domain or manor, but this work was usually done by his steward or bailiff. In later years, the senior knights, keepers of castles, had more developed duties in the administration of the law and the keeping of the peace, sitting as local judges and, particularly in England and Germany, often having a duty to keep the peace beyond the confines of their feudal domain.

▲ *Courtly banquets were designed to impress, with lavish displays of food and drink.*

◄ *Home and feudal stronghold – the castle of a great lord dominated the country for miles around. Pontefract Castle in west Yorkshire, shown here, was founded in c.1070. It was greatly developed by John of Gaunt and was the scene of King Richard II's murder.*

A LORD IN HIS MANOR
A KNIGHT'S RIGHTS AND DUTIES AT HOME

Knighthood did not necessarily bring a large estate with it. Some knights were in possession of fiefs too small to support them adequately and exploited their military training and skill to make a living through tournaments and on the field of battle by ransoming defeated enemies. But ideally a great knight was master of a substantial landholding.

THE NOBILITY OF LORDSHIP
A great knight was lord to a large number of retainers and lived in great style. This was seen as proper in the chivalric world. Ramon Llull wrote in his *Book of the Order of Chivalry* that knights rightly should be 'made lord of many men, for in seignory is much nobleness'. A lord would take pride in seeing his retainers wearing his arms on their clothing. The larger the household, the greater the glory.

Medieval philosophers held that feudal society was divided into three estates or conditions: the Church was the first estate; the nobility, the knights and lords who held feudal properties were members of

▼ *The main hall of a medieval castle was its central public space, where a lord would eat, dispense justice and entertain.*

▲ *Peasants build a fence on their lord's land while in the background one of their fellows ploughs a field on the farm.*

the second; and the peasantry was the third. It was proper, ordained by God, that the members of the third estate should labour to support the members of the other two. Another image, developed by lawyers in the late medieval period, was that society rightly ordered was like a great pyramid, with the peasants at the bottom, the clergy above them and the knights beneath the king at the top. Above the

king was only God himself, and this social structure – in which each man knew his place – was believed to have been blessed and to be sustained by God.

GOVERNOR OF THE MANOR
Under the system introduced in England by the Normans, and current in much of western and central Europe, the knight's landholding as a feudal lord was called a manor, or in France a *seigneurie*. The feudal lord (*seigneur*) had legal and economic power within his manor.

Typically, a manor contained a village and arable and pasture land farmed in strips by the lord's tenants. Some of the land was the lord's and some was farmed on their own behalf by the peasants. The peasants had to farm the lord's lands and in addition had to pay 'taxes', usually 'in kind' in the form of a proportion of the agricultural produce grown on their own strips of land. The lord had duties and

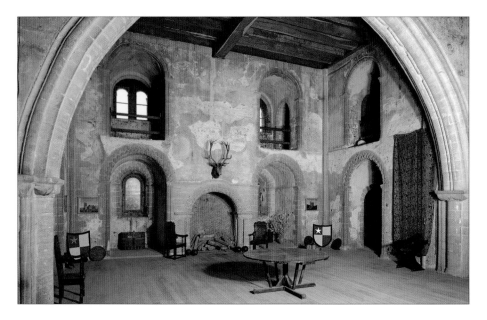

responsibilities to govern his tenants. He presided at a manor court. His manor was a self-sufficient community.

The fief-holder supported by his land tenants could be a secular knight or a prominent clergyman such as a bishop or abbot. Many bishops and abbots were knights, and fought in feudal armies. The feudal households described in this chapter could be secular or ecclesiastical.

A NOBLE HOUSEHOLD

From the 12th century, a leading knight's household would contain a range of administrative positions. The *seneschal*, or steward, was in overall charge of food and drink for his lord, while the butler managed its storage. The chamberlain was guardian and manager of the lord's private chambers and their contents, with the help of subordinate valets and janitors. The priest was likely to be one of the few literate people in the castle: he ran the chapel, said religious services and kept the lord's written records in order. The constable and marshal oversaw the security of the castle, and managed the garrison and other troops as well as overseeing the running of the mews and stables.

Among those who provided service to a king or great lord were powerful knights. Chivalry honoured service; there was nothing demeaning about it. In Arthurian literature, King Arthur's seneschal was Sir Kay, who was one of the knights of the Round Table. This arrangement was typical of the period. Knights might provide service in the hall, the stables, the tilt-yard, the armoury and the hunting park. Such was the size of these feudal households that lords with grand positions such as Marshal or Master of the Horse had many more menial staff beneath them. Some of the lower positions were filled by squires.

Those knights and noblemen who occupied elite positions in the inner household were free to offer advice to the lord they served, both as individuals, and gathered together in council. The lord might disregard their opinions, just as the king could go against the will of his

barons, as happened frequently – notably in 13th-century England, under King John and King Henry III.

SPECIALIZATION OF ROLES

During the 13th–15th centuries, the roles of officials in the larger noble households became more specialized and titles were changed. In the 13th century the treasurer took charge of finances, while the role of steward was divided in two, with one managing the lord's estates and tenants and a second in charge of food and provisions. In the 14th century this position was often called the chamberlain, while a clerk managed the butler's store of food.

In a large household of the 15th century, the seneschal was often the lord's deputy, in charge of key roles such as the dispensing of justice when the lord was absent – as he frequently was, either at another of his manors or on campaign.

▲ *A feudal estate was a self-sufficient unit, in which each person had a role and a strictly defined social position.*

The seneschal was assisted by a chancellor, responsible for keeping administrative documents, writing letters, charters and legal papers. By this time the chamberlain often focused mainly on financial affairs, while the steward managed the estate. The highest authority in the lord's absence was the constable, who was the 'keeper' of the castle and responsible for its defence.

KEEPING A GRAND HOUSE

It was honourable for a feudal lord to entertain men of rank. Even a prince could enhance his status by offering hospitality to a knight. Llull declared that: 'Any baron or lord who honours a knight in his court, in his meetings of council and at his meals does honour to himself'.

KEEPER OF THE PEACE

A KNIGHT'S ROLE IN GOVERNMENT

As feudalism developed, many knights across Europe accepted it as their duty to maintain order in peacetime and to administer the king's law. The knights and their castle strongholds became symbols of a stern authority that demanded respect and kept lawlessness at bay.

JURY SERVICE

By the mid-13th century many leading English knights were no longer simply a warrior caste in the king's service, but were part of the royal administration. They had a major role in delivering justice, both local and national. As we have seen, they presided over manorial courts; they also had to provide jury members for grand assize – the travelling royal court held periodically in English counties. This jury work involved, in addition to attending the hearings, demanding administrative work and in criminal cases law enforcement duties. Such duties were not taken

on by all knights, and those members of the chivalric class who did shoulder these responsibilities shared them with other nobles who were not knights.

▲ *The king's law had to be administered as well as enforced around the country and knights contributed to the work of travelling courts that brought justice to the shires.*

Some knights had a similar role in France and Germany. In France some made a good living as administrators for the king, for these tasks were well paid there. In Germany *ministeriales* were 'serf-knights' who worked mainly as stewards, judges and administrators. Originally the *ministeriales* were not free men, since they were tied to the land on which they served and were without legal rights beyond that domain. But they gradually acquired the right to own property and generate wealth, and in time became members of the knightly class, with the right to hold fiefdoms in the gift of other lords in addition to their original suzerain.

KNIGHTS OF THE SHIRE

In the 13th century English knights attended the royal council that was the precursor to Parliament. Two knights from each shire were summoned to the governmental council called by English

---

SYMBOL OF ORDER

In chivalric literature the castle is frequently a symbol of order. Within its walls, and on the feudal estate, all is well – the lord and his retainers live in comfort, each knowing his place and providing service. Outside the island of order are all the terrors of an unruly world – symbolized in chivalric literature by the forest, with its monsters and rogue knights. The medieval world had a fear of disorder – raids by Vikings, Magyars and Saracens were still fresh in folk memory. The castle's structures and discipline would keep the darkness of the forest at bay, while the structures of feudal society guaranteed social order.

▼ *Leeds Castle, Kent, begun in 1119.*

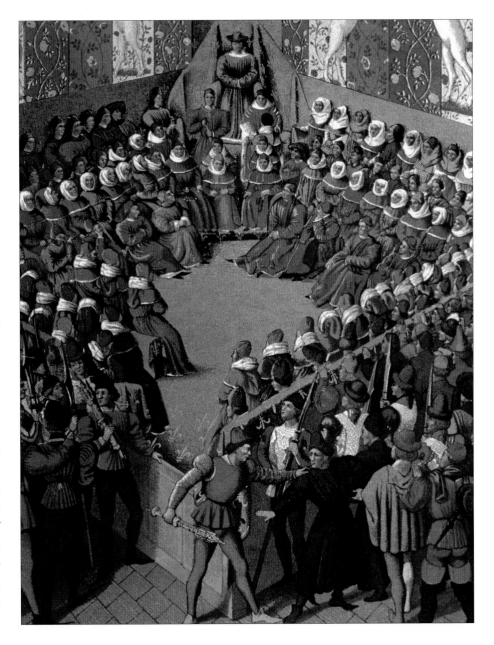

▶ *A convocation of lords enforces the power of the French monarchy, hearing the trial of John II, duke of Alençon, for treason against Charles VII. Alençon was sentenced to death in 1458 but the sentence was not carried out; he died in prison in 1476.*

nobleman Simon de Montfort when he was briefly in power in 1263–65, having deposed King Henry III. De Montfort was then defeated and killed by Henry III's son, the future Edward I, at the Battle of Evesham and his experiment ended, but it had set a precedent. In 1295 Edward I called a representative council later termed the 'Model Parliament' by historians, because it was the first representative English parliament.

The Model Parliament included, in addition to magnates and churchmen, representatives of lesser clergy, two knights from each county, two burgesses from each borough and two citizens from every city. The council began to be called Parliament (from the old French *parlement*, 'a talk') at around this time, and in the reign of King Edward III (1327–77) split into its current format: the House of Commons and the House of Lords. At that point, the knights of the shire, the lesser clergy and the burgesses formed the House of Commons, while the nobles and high clergy formed the House of Lords.

PROTECTORS OF THE WEAK

All knights also had a general duty to provide protection for the Church, widows, children and others unable to protect themselves. In the writings of philosophers and churchmen, knights' elevated position within the feudal system was justified by this role as protectors.

Knights had a particular duty to protect pilgrims. Pilgrimage played a central role in religious life in the Middle Ages. As an act of penance or an expression of Christian devotion, men and women uprooted themselves and travelled along the well-worn routes to shrines such as Canterbury, Santiago de Compostela in Spain, Rome and Jerusalem. They

travelled in large numbers: as early as 1064 a party of 7,000 travelled to Jerusalem, which at this stage was in Muslim hands. After the First Crusade in 1096–99 resulted in the recapture of Jerusalem, the number of pilgrims to the Holy Land increased further. All pilgrimages could be dangerous, but the voyage to Jerusalem was particularly long and difficult. The knightly brotherhood of the Knights Templar was established in *c.*1119 to protect pilgrims to the Holy Land.

THE EXPRESSION OF LORDSHIP

The castle was an expression in stone of the knight's mastery and authority. Many castles were built around a great central

tower or keep, known as the *donjon*, a French word derived from the Latin *dominium*, meaning lordship. (The English equivalent is 'dungeon'; this word did not come to have its modern meaning, of a dank underground jail room, until later.)

Even when the knight was not in residence – as was often the case, when he was away on campaign, or perhaps visiting another of his residences – the forbidding walls of his castle proclaimed both the greatness of the knight and the solidity of the rule of law that he enforced. The castle was a standing warning to law breakers of the military might that could be brought against them if they rebelled against the lord's authority.

CASTLES AND MANOR HOUSES

LIFE ON A FEUDAL ESTATE

Castles were military instruments, used as bases for expansion and afterwards for dominating conquered territory, but they were also domestic environments. They were a show of power, and a statement of authority, but were also knightly residences, set at the heart of great feudal estates or manors.

EVERYTHING A LORD NEEDED

The great estates were virtually self-sufficient. The castle or fortified house was surrounded by pasture and crop fields, with hundreds of peasants working the land to produce corn and hay, raising animals for the lord's table and chopping the wood needed for fires. On some estates even the cloth worn by the lord and his household was woven on site, but if not, wool produced by sheep on the estate was taken to a nearby centre to be exchanged or woven.

Anything that could not be produced on the estate – salt, say, or iron goods – could be purchased from itinerant merchants or at fairs held in the larger market towns. Larger fairs attracted merchants from as far away as Italy, France and Germany, some selling goods all the way from the far eastern countries of the Muslim world. At the larger markets, a lord's household staff could buy spices, gold, silks, dyes, French or Spanish wine, furs, Flemish cloth and so on.

AN EMPTY HOME

Kings in this period had to keep mobile in order to keep themselves abreast of developments and to maintain their authority. They carried their court with them as they travelled from household to household. Likewise, princes and the greater lords had more than one castle and moved from one to another. Much of their wealth consisted

of land, and its produce, paid to them as rents-in-kind. As the court, and lesser lords, moved from one property to another, their rents – in the form of harvested food and hunted animals – kept them and their courtiers well fed.

When they were away at another house, or indeed on campaign or crusade, the castle was guarded and administered by a castellan, or governor, with a defensive garrison of knights and crossbowmen alongside a team of artisans such as carpenters, smiths and masons to maintain the buildings. The peasants working the estate would of course stay where they were, but the majority of the lord's household would travel with him – necessarily, for they would be needed to provide service in the next location.

DEFENSIVE DESIGNS

Castles took many forms, designed primarily for defence. The Normans who pioneered castle-building often built to a 'motte and bailey' design: the motte was an artificial or natural mound within or adjacent to a wider area called the bailey, set inside a defensive wall and ditch or moat. On the motte stood a tower – made of wood in early castles, later of stone – which usually housed the lord's living quarters and that was a stronghold to which the lord and his garrison could retreat if the castle came under attack and the outer defences were breached.

Later castle-builders – in England and Wales, most notably King Edward I and his builder Master James of St Georges – improved upon this basic pattern. The

◀ *The hall at Penshurst Place, a fortified manor house in Kent, southern England, was completed in 1341. A medieval hall was a space that the lord shared with his retainers, guests and animals. It would be noisy, crowded and full of smoke from the central fire.*

▲ *The kitchens were generally just off the main hall. Often a carved wooden screen disguised the passageway that led from the hall to the larders, kitchens and offices.*

▲ *Banquets were seen by noble households as an opportunity to display wealth and influence, and they would be as lavish and impressive as possible.*

perfection of medieval fortress design was the concentric castle that had two sets of walls: a taller inner set, surrounding the 'inner bailey', and a lower outer set, surrounding the 'outer bailey'. To capture a concentric castle, attackers would have first to defeat the defenders of the outer walls, then cross the outer bailey under fire and begin their assault on the inner, more heavily fortified walls. Fine examples of the concentric castle include the Krak des Chevaliers (near Homs in Syria) which was built and garrisoned by

▼ *This view of Salzburg in 1493 shows how the medieval castle and the fortified cathedral – symbols of the dual powers of State and Church – dominate the city.*

the Knights Hospitaller during the Crusades, and Beaumaris Castle in North Wales built by Edward I and Master James of St Georges.

DOMESTIC BUILDINGS

The large empty baileys or yards that we see in many castles today were once filled with domestic buildings. These were usually constructed of wattle and daub or timber and were either destroyed in conflict or have decayed naturally. They would have included stables, an armoury, a smithy, a servants' hall, the kitchens and the buttery (a storeroom for wines, so called because casks of wine were called butts). In some castles, certain of these halls and rooms were built into the walls surrounding the bailey and so their remains can still be viewed.

The lord of a great castle would have lavish accommodation. His rooms were always in the safest part of the fortress –

initially in the keep or donjon, then, as castle design developed, in the strongly fortified inner bailey. Also in the inner bailey, close to the lord's rooms, would be the chapel and the great hall, the centre of castle life. Even the greatest lord would eat with his retainers in the hall. Robert Grosseteste, scholar and Bishop of Lincoln under King Henry III of England, wrote that it was not proper for a lord to eat alone.

The lord, his family, companions and notable visitors would eat at the high table on finer foods than were served to the mass of soldiers and other vassals in the main part of the room. At the far end of the hall, opposite the high table, was often a raised minstrels' gallery from where musicians entertained diners. In between meals the hall was also a place of business used for judicial hearings and estate management, and by night many of the castle's large population slept there.

Some castles contained more than one chapel. In the lord's private chapel, he and his family would attend a service each morning. A larger chapel in the outer bailey would serve the needs of the members of the garrison. Many castles had a heavily fortified gatehouse guarding the entrance. This usually contained rooms for the castellan, and perhaps a smaller version of the great hall used for receiving visitors and emissaries.

SALCZBVRGA

KNIGHTS AT LEISURE
FAVOURED PASTIMES OF THE CHIVALRIC CLASS

Knights had duties both in peace and in war, but they also had plenty of time for leisure. They spent much of this time in pursuits that improved their military skill or their understanding of their knightly calling, although they were also fond of lavish feasts.

THE HUNT

Hunting provided a key opportunity for developing fitness and strength and practising horsemanship as well as the skilled use of weapons such as the bow and arrow, the spear and the sword. The *Anglo-Saxon Chronicle* reports that King William I of England enclosed vast tracts of forest and 'loved the tall stags as if he were father unto them'. The 13th-century English chronicler William Rishanger, a Benedictine monk from St Albans also known as Chronigraphus, described how as a young man Prince Edward (the future warrior-king Edward I) loved to hunt stags on horseback, and when he had chased one down he would kill it at close quarters with his sword rather than from a safe distance with a spear. This was presented as a sign of his bravery and martial spirit.

Manuals on hunting were circulated to complement the handbooks on chivalry. The French nobleman Count Gaston III of Foix-Béarn wrote a treatise on hunting, *Le Livre de Chasse* ('The Book of the Hunt') *c*.1387. Gaston was a great chivalric figure, who wrote that the three main delights of his life were 'arms, love, and hunting', and whose court in southern France was described in all its knightly splendour by French chronicler Jean Froissart. *Le Livre de Chasse* covered all aspects of hunting in the 14th century, listing the open and close seasons for animals, the best kinds of bait and traps to use, the different kinds of pursuit, including a discussion of which hounds to use for which animal, and even ideal arrangements for dining in the forest.

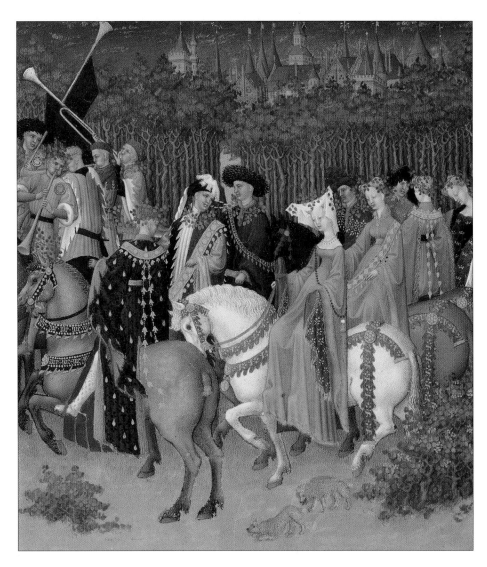

▲ *A hunting party gathers outside the castle walls. Ladies often rode on the hunt alongside men. Hunting dogs were used to track, chase and kill prey; greyhounds were particularly prized for their speed.*

HUNTING RESERVES

Kings, noblemen and leading knights kept hunting reserves that were strictly guarded. The *Anglo-Saxon Chronicle* reports that William I imposed blinding as the punishment for anyone who killed deer from his forests. They employed specialists to care for the lands, maintain the wild animals and look after the hounds. Hunting was considered a noble pastime and positions involving the management of horse, hounds or the hunt were quite appropriate ones for a knight to take in the household of his feudal superior. The nobles developed a hierarchy among the animals: the noblest target was the stag, then, in descending order, the boar, the female deer, the wolf and the bear, the fox and the hare.

HAWKING

Another favoured pastime of the royal and knightly class was hawking, the use of trained birds of prey such as eagles, falcons and hawks to pursue game. Some contemporary sources suggest that the crusader knights learned of the sport in the Holy Land and brought it back to

Tancarville, Chamberlain of Normandy, Marshal was nicknamed *gaste-viande* ('glutton') for, unless otherwise occupied, he filled every waking hour with eating. But the biography makes clear that this was no indication of slothfulness and laziness, noting that de Tancarville predicted a great future for the young man. Likewise in one romance, English knight Guy de Bourgogne made quite an impact on the Saracens merely with his appetite, which was said to be equivalent to that of four normal men – and he demonstrated the general truth that 'a man who eats heartily will never prove to be a coward'.

As many as ten courses would be served on a great occasion. These included such dishes as boar, swan, peacock, fowl, fish, cheese, fruit and pastries, with plenty of wine, cider, spiced mead and sometimes beer to keep spirits high. A medieval document that lists the 'Fifteen Joys of a Knight' identifies the first and foremost of these joys as 'eating well and going swiftly through the supplies of wine'.

Music was usually played by minstrels during the meal and afterwards knights might play at dice or chess. But their favourite after-dinner event was a recitation by a travelling minstrel of *chansons de geste* or *chansons d'amour*, accounts of great

▲ *Minstrels were generally employed at the castle, but the troubadours who sang songs of courtly love were wandering musicians.*

Europe, but there is evidence to suggest that in fact it was practised by both Anglo-Saxon and Norman lords before that time. In the 1240s Holy Roman Emperor Frederick II was the patron for a translation of an Arabic treatise on hunting with birds, and he then wrote a book himself on the subject – incorporating some of the translated Arab text and supplementing it with information gleaned from his own lifelong devotion to the sport.

FEASTING AND POETRY

Days could be long in the castle. A favourite way to pass the time was in feasting and drinking. A vast appetite was not considered inappropriate for a great knight – indeed, it was almost a virtue, a sign of a warrior virility and forcefulness. The verse biography of 12th-century English knight William Marshal reveals that in his youth when he was serving as a squire in the household of his uncle, William de

▶ *Chivalric tournaments provided much excitement and colour. A Dutch illumination of c.1475 represents knights and ladies riding through the streets of London to a tournament.*

▲ *Chess was invented in India and spread via the Arab world to Europe by c.1000. It was so popular among the nobility that it became known as the 'royal game'.*

knightly doings in battle or romances of courtly love. The 'Fifteen Joys of a Knight' indicates that a knight would always show hospitality to a wandering poet. In this way the knight was sustained in his daily life by the poems and romances of chivalry, which functioned as a mythology of knighthood.

MARRIAGES AND ALLIANCES
THE INCREASING IMPORTANCE OF SOCIAL STANDING

Knights dreamed of doing the great chivalric deeds described in the many chansons, and some had the excitement of riding out on heroic campaigns and fighting great battles, but they also lived in the day-to-day world of social and financial obligations. In this world a knight's standing and that of his family could be a pressing concern.

In the higher levels of feudal society occupied by knights, marriages were normally based on considerations of social standing and wealth, and marital engagements were arranged in order to acquire property or to make a political alliance with a powerful lord. A good marriage for a knight or his daughters could bring with it great landholdings.

THE ROLL OF ARMS
Knights of this era rode into battle and into tournaments bearing their coat of arms on their shield, surcoat or other tunic and horsecloths. These coats of arms developed from simple symbols worn by early knights to identify themselves in battle, and gradually became more complex. When a knight acquired new lands through marriage a new title and coat of arms would come with them; he would then add the new 'arms' to his own coat of arms. In battles and particularly at tournaments heralds were the experts on these arms. A herald might work for a great lord and have jurisdiction throughout the area of his power: he would keep a 'roll of arms' listing the different coats of arms for all the knights in the area.

WILLIAM MARSHAL'S RISE
The great 12th-century English knight William Marshal was the model for those needing to better themselves. He rose from relatively humble origins to be the equal of the leading knights and nobles by dint of his prowess in tournaments and on the field of battle. From a position where, as a junior knight in the house of William de Tancarville, he had to sell his clothes to buy a new horse, he achieved such status within the world of chivalry that in 1189 he married one of the richest women in England, the 17-year-old Isabel de Clare, heiress to Richard de Clare, 2nd Earl of Pembroke. Marshal was made earl and he went on to become Marshal of England and Protector of the Kingdom in the minority of King Henry III.

DAUGHTERS OF A POOR KNIGHT
A rise such as Marshal's was an inspiring dream, of course, but also an exception to the rule. Many knights lived in relatively straitened circumstances, and found it difficult to maintain a good position for themselves and their families in the world of the noble elite. Impoverished or struggling knights were common figures in the literature of chivalry.

In the 12th-century Spanish epic poem *Cantar del Mio Cid* ('Song of the Cid'), the poem's hero, great Spanish warrior Don

◄ A roll of arms of Yorkshire lords, recorded in c.1483 by William Ballard, March King of Arms under the English kings Edward IV and Richard III.

▲ *Philip the Bold, Duke of Burgundy, made a highly advantageous alliance when he married Marguerite, Countess of Flanders, in 1369, after which he became Count of Flanders and of Artois.*

Rodrigo Diaz de Vivar ('El Cid') goes to war in part to provide for his family. He needs to furnish his daughters with suitable dowries, and to find fitting husbands for them. He achieves his aim by raising tribute from Muslim leaders, capturing Valencia and giving his daughters in marriage to the kings of Navarre and Aragon.

In the Arthurian romance *Érec et Énide* ('Eric and Enid') by the 12th-century French poet Chrétien de Troyes, the Lady Enid's father is a knight fallen on hard times, who is too poor to provide a dowry for her or to dress her in finery. Enid is ashamed of her worn clothes, but her father is not a figure of ridicule in the poem: he is presented as pleasing, generous, forthright, attractive – he possesses the virtues of a good knight, despite being poor. The plight of his family is presented with sympathy.

Chivalric literature describes the interaction of the ideal code of chivalry with the real world. According to the code, knightly virtues matter far more than worldly wealth, but the poems make clear that there may be unpleasant consequences of failing to acquire wealth alongside virtue.

CHIVALRIC WEDDINGS

Within noble society, marriages were celebrated with all the trappings of chivalry. Some of the greatest of medieval tournaments were held as celebrations of the weddings of noble lords or their daughters. In 1359 the wedding of John of Gaunt to Blanche of Lancaster at Reading was marked by a tournament in which King Edward III, his sons and 19 other nobles entered the lists clad as the mayor and aldermen of London, and fought against all comers.

▶ *Extravagant gestures and declarations of love were an integral part of the social interaction of a court. Attachments were made to single and married women alike.*

LOVE AT COURT

In a world in which marriages were made principally in the light of considerations of political expedience or property holdings, love may have seemed like a luxury. Some matrimonial matches began as diplomatic arrangements but became deeply loving. For example, the marriage of the future Edward I of England and Eleanor of Castile started as a diplomatic alliance when he was 15 years old and she was only nine, but ended as a powerful relationship, honoured by Edward after the queen's death in 1290 with the erection of 12 memorial crosses marking the spots at which her funeral cortége stopped on its route from her place of death at Harby, in Nottinghamshire, and her place of burial, Westminster Abbey in London. (Charing Cross in central London is a replica of one of these memorials.) In mourning, Edward wrote: 'In life I dearly loved her and I will not stop loving her in death'.

These deeply loving matches were, however, exceptions to the general rule. The cult of courtly love gave an outlet to romantic passion within the chivalric world. The lady to whom knights would dedicate their service in the courtly love tradition was usually already married to a great lord. The knight may have felt a deep passion for her on account of the connection, and may have expressed his longing for physical union with his beloved, yet very few of the relationships celebrated in these poems would have come to physical consummation.

LIFE IN A KNIGHTLY BROTHERHOOD
DAY-TO-DAY LIFE FOR A KNIGHT TEMPLAR OR A HOSPITALLER

Like other knights, the members of the great chivalric brotherhoods such as the Knights Hospitaller and the Knights Templar also spent periods 'at home', away from the excitement and difficulties of life on the battlefield. For much of the time, they lived a life not unlike that of the monks in Cistercian or Benedictine houses.

Those joining up to military orders took the monastic vows of poverty, chastity and obedience. (One brotherhood, the Spanish Order of Santiago, allowed married men to join.) Mostly the brothers lived a communal existence, in quarters designed like those in a conventional monastery, eating in a refectory and sleeping in a dormitory. They followed the monastic hours and were required to attend services.

The monks were largely lay brethren, many of them illiterate. In addition, there were literate clerical brothers who would serve as chaplains and recite the services or daily offices while the others listened. A typical rule required the lay brothers to repeat the *pater noster* (the Lord's Prayer), a number of times at each of the set offices.

▼ *Krak des Chevaliers, a fortress originally built in 1031 for the Emir of Aleppo, was given to the Knights Hospitaller in 1144, who rebuilt it as the largest crusader castle in the Levant.*

▲ *The Templars wore Christ's cross into battle on clothing, shields and horse coverings. Their full name was 'Poor Fellow-Soldiers of Christ and of the Temple of Solomon'.*

A NOBLE CALLING

It was not an easy life for the knights of these brotherhoods. The address or statement read out before an applicant to the Hospitaller order made it clear that he would have to be willing to sacrifice his own desires and needs and devote himself to the service of the order. It said that to enter the order was a great and noble calling, but that he should not expect to have a magnificent steed or to be kept in comfort. It said that he would find that when he wanted to sleep, the order might require him to be on watch, and when he wanted to eat he might have to fast. The knight would have to be able and willing to travel far away, 'to places that will not be pleasing', and that he would often find it necessary 'to abandon [his] desires in order to fulfil those of another'.

MILITARY RANKS

In the principal knightly orders, the lay brothers were divided into two ranks: sergeants and knights. There were two kinds of sergeant: non-fighting sergeants and sergeants-at-arms. In the monastery the sergeants performed necessary farming and household work, but the knights were of higher rank and were spared this labour. The brothers undertook military exercises to keep themselves prepared for war. Knights had better armour and three or four horses, while sergeants-at-arms made do with basic protection and only a single horse. The sergeants would sometimes fight as infantry alongside their brother-knights. The brothers in the different orders built or repaired and garrisoned many castles.

RULES OF LIVING

The warrior-monks followed a less strict diet than that of their contemporaries in the non-military orders. They were allowed to eat meat, normally on three days a week, in order to keep up their strength for military activities.

Other rules were very strict. Most orders required silence at mealtimes. The favourite leisure activities of secular knights, such as hunting, hawking and fighting in tournaments, were all outlawed – although, as we shall see in Chapter Five, brothers in the Knights Templar were

allowed to take part in *bohorts*, the form of tournament in which there was no physical conflict, presumably as a way of maintaining their fitness and good horsemanship. Another exception to the general rule was made in the case of the brothers of the Spanish military order of Calatrava, who lived in a barren landscape, and were allowed to hunt in order to secure food.

There were strict rules on clothing, which should normally be plain and of

▲ *In 1347–48, the Knights Hospitallers, by then based on Rhodes and known as the Knights of Rhodes, came to the aid of King Constantine III of Armenian Cilicia in his conflict with the Mamluk Sultan of Egypt.*

wool. It appears that these kinds of rules may have been honoured more in the breach than in the observance – in the 13th century the statutes of the Knights Hospitallers often found it necessary to denounce the use of embroidery on any clothing and even of silver and gold adornment on military equipment. The Templars allowed the brothers in Syria to wear linen, rather than wool, in the hot summer months.

In many of the orders, there was no probationary period or novitiate of the kind followed in the non-military orders. This must have made it difficult to establish whether applicants were really suited to the communal life of the brotherhood. The strict rules were enforced with fierce penalties, which ranged from being expelled to receiving a beating or merely being asked to perform a few days of penitential activities.

YOUNGER SONS

In feudal society property was inherited by the oldest son, which generally made it difficult for younger sons to make their way in the world. At one time, historians argued that many of these relatively poor younger sons went on crusade seeking their fortune, but modern scholars have stressed the enormous expense and financial risk of travelling on crusade and argued that normally only the wealthy could have made the decision to take the cross and become a crusader. The orders of warrior-monks, however, offered a way in which younger sons and even the children of non-noble families could make a career as a knight; up to the mid-13th century applicants from outside the nobility were able to enter the brotherhoods. There they received very good military training. Their financial position probably meant that they would not have been able to marry outside the order, so that they were not giving up the chance of a wedded life when they took the order's vow of chastity.

CHAPTER FOUR

A KNIGHT AT ARMS

Mounted knights riding with couched lances in cavalry charges, and wielding mace and sword in close combat, dominate popular visions of battles in the age of chivalry. In reality the exploits of individual knights were usually far less important than we may think in determining the outcome of battles. Accounts in poems, romances and even chronicles were written to praise and memorialize feats of arms by knights, and they exaggerated the number who fought and their importance in battle.

These accounts also overplayed the importance of battles themselves. Pitched battles were rare in the Middle Ages and wars were often conducted through a series of sieges with attacking armies trying to draw out their opponents. However, knights were occasionally the difference between victory and defeat on the battlefield. A celebrated example of such a conflict is the Battle of Bouvines, northern France, on 27 July 1214, in which Philip IV of France was victorious over a German–Flemish army led by Holy Roman Emperor Otto IV. The battle was fought on a front over a mile long, with three areas of fighting: on the two wings and in the centre, where initially the Flemish infantry got the upper hand, but the French recovered and Philip led the cavalry charge. The battle was decided in this central area between the two groups of mounted knights, with daggers and swords. Otto was unhorsed and his imperial standard was captured, but he was saved from capture by the bravery of a group of Saxon knights.

▲ *The reality of medieval warfare involved plunder and looting.*

◄ *After the brutal clash of armies in battle, courtesy was restored in ransom and peace talks. This chivalric encounter is the aftermath of Philip IV's victory at Bouvines in 1214.*

THE MOUNTED WARRIOR
A KNIGHT IN BATTLE

The mounted warriors who fought alongside Duke William of Normandy at the Battle of Hastings in 1066 wore chain mail coats that extended to the knees and the elbows, and were split at the sides and front to make it easier to move. On their heads the warriors wore a conical metal helmet with a single downward protrusion to protect the nose. They carried a long shield shaped like a kite, which when used on horseback offered them protection from head to toe.

▼ *The Norman knights of the 10th and 11th centuries would be dressed in chain mail, which made mounting and dismounting possible in the thick of battle.*

CHAIN MAIL
The basic chain mail tunic (hauberk) or long robe (byrnie), made of circular interlocking links of iron, had changed little since the time of Charlemagne, and continued as the basic defensive armour until the end of the 13th century. Additions were made to it to increase protection. These included a chain mail hood (camail or coif); a chain mail mouth flap (ventail) to protect the lower face; chain mail mittens; and quilted cuisses with metal sewn in to protect the upper legs.

CHARGING WITH A LANCE
Anna Comnena, daughter of Byzantine emperor Alexius Comnenus, was powerfully impressed by the impact of charging crusader knights, which she witnessed at Byzantium in 1096–97. She wrote that the 'first shock' was 'irresistible' and conjectured that they could 'make a hole in the walls of Babylon'. Chronicle accounts may exaggerate the importance of knights in determining the outcome of battles, but there is no denying the force of mounted, armoured knights at full charge.

The knights described by Anna Comnena were charging in a coordinated unit with couched lance. This manoeuvre was developed in the second half of the 11th century in northern France – probably by the Normans. It is a key technique of the age of chivalry, seen both in the lists at tournaments and on the field of battle.

▲ *Norman knights charge at the Battle of Hastings. They use their lances as spears rather than 'couched' under the right arm.*

Mounted soldiers, dressed in chain mail in earlier armies, had used the lance as a spear for overarm throwing when mounted, and for jabbing when fighting on the ground. Knights, however, learned to hold the lance firmly beneath their arm and use it as a weapon of impact. The full force of the knight's charge was delivered at the point of impact, and the knight retained his lance, so that after a charge he could wheel away with the weapon and charge again. Another advantage of the new technique was that the knights could use a heavier lance, because they did not have to lift the weapon up to throw it or jab with it. Lances kept the enemy at a distance, making a knight less vulnerable.

A MIGHTY CHALLENGE
Handling both horse and weapons on the battlefield was extremely difficult. A knight needed to have the ability to control the horse when riding at speed, and when changing direction, through a crowded field if necessary. The knight would be quickly despatched if he were not physically fit and highly skilled in the use of his mount and equipment. For this reason, chivalric literature stressed repeatedly the need for knights to train in the arts of war: tournaments provided an

SADDLE AND STIRRUP

Warriors rode horses in battle for centuries before the solid saddle and the stirrups made them secure on their mounts. The Assyrian cavalry developed the first saddle in about 800–700BC. It was no more than a simple cloth tied around the horse, giving the rider a better grip. The Scythians used an improved, padded saddle. The Nubian mercenaries in the Roman army used a solid saddle built high at the front (pommel) and back (cantle). Of partic-

ular relevance for the massed charge was the use of a high pommel, invaluable for helping the knight to stay mounted at the shuddering moment of impact.

Stirrups made the rider much more secure and allowed him to fight energetically. It is not known for sure when and where the stirrup was invented. Around 500BC, soldiers in India were using a simple leather loop, and the Sarmatians – nomadic contemporaries of the Scythians – used one stirrup-like loop as a help in mounting. The oldest evidence for the use of twin stirrups, one on each side, was in an ancient Chinese tomb of AD322.

From their use by the nomadic groups from Asia, notably the Avars who rode into what is now Hungary, stirrups were gradually adopted in Europe, and more generally by the 8th century.

◀ *An early pair of Avarian stirrups from the 8th century.*

essential opportunity to practise, in addition to being an opportunity for self-display and courtly manoeuvring.

A knight could not have fought like this without specialized weapons and equipment. Probably most important of all to the effectiveness of mounted warfare were the saddle and stirrups. Also relevant is that horseshoes were developed in the late 11th century. Horses with horseshoes could travel farther and cross rougher country than those without them.

SWORD AND LANCE

A mounted warrior in the early Middle Ages carried a light sword, weighing less than 1.5kg (3lb), which he used mainly for cutting and slashing. From the 11th and 12th centuries, the sword was usually a little longer with a sharper point so he could thrust with it as well. In the late 13th century a typical knight's sword had a blade of 80cm (2ft 6in) with a handle of

around 20cm (8in). In the following century they used a two-handed broadsword that was almost twice as long, measuring 1.8m (6ft) in total.

All sword handles (hilts) featured a cross-guard, a pair of extensions (quillions) at the blade end of the handle that prevented the hand sliding off the handle. Sometimes knights would reverse the sword when fighting – holding the sword by the covered blade they used the quillions to undermine an opponent's balance

by knocking his knee or ankle. At the end of the hilt was the pommel, a heavy rounded extension, which could also be used as a weapon.

In the late 13th century knights fought with a lance around 2.4m (8ft) in length, and 14th-century lances became longer still – typically 3m (10ft). The spearhead was strong enough to pierce armour.

DAGGER AND MACE

In close combat knights also used daggers and one-handed battle-axes. One type of dagger had a straight blade with a single cutting edge, and was called a misericorde from the Latin *misericordia* ('mercy') because it was used to finish off a badly wounded knight – perhaps by stabbing through the helmet visor or under the gorget. Another dagger was the anelace, a broad double-edged tapering dagger with a blade of up to 45cm (18in).

A knight could also attack a nearby opponent by hitting him with a mace – a wooden club with a metal or stone head. A blow from a mace was often enough to stun an opponent and was the favoured weapon of clerics in battle, for while they were expected to fight, they were not supposed to shed blood. Some spiked maces, such as the flanged mace and morning star mace, could penetrate armour.

The battle-axe was an effective weapon when used with force: at the Battle of Bannockburn, Robert the Bruce reputedly killed the knight Sir Henry de Bohun with a single blow to his head.

▼ *From top: battle-axe, 'morning star' mace, anelace dagger and broadsword.*

THE ARMOURED KNIGHT

PROTECTION IN BATTLE

The main advantages of chain mail were that it was not too heavy and allowed considerable freedom of movement. However, it could not stop the point of a lance or the edge of a sword. In the 12th century, knights began to wear a padded jerkin beneath the mail, which

▼ *In the 13th century knights began to wear pieces of metal plate armour in conjunction with chain mail. The leg piece is jointed just below the knee for ease of movement.*

helped to absorb the shock of blows, but was still easily penetrated. In addition, a heavy blow, even if it did not break the mail, could force pieces of chain into the wound, making injury and bleeding worse. Chain mail was also difficult to clean and keep rust-free.

THE 'COAT OF ARMS'

The custom of wearing a surcoat, a cloth garment worn over the chain mail, was probably brought back by the crusaders from the Holy Land, where they learned its use from Muslim armies. Soldiers and knights – both in battle and at tournaments – wore coats of arms on their surcoats as a means of identification.

SUITS OF ARMOUR

The first steps towards suits of solid plate armour were taken in the 13th century. Initially chest and back plates of hardened leather were tried, and small pieces of solid metal were attached to the chain mail suit at the elbows, armpits and knees. The next stage was to attach jointed plates of metal to a leather base, making a jacket for the entire upper body.

The first suits of armour in *c.*1330 consisted of many pieces, often connected by complex lacing, which together provided layered protection for the body. It took a long time to put a suit like this on, and there are several accounts of knights being unprepared if an army was surprised.

These suits were gradually improved to counter the devastating effects of the longbow and the crossbow. The breastplate was introduced in the late 1300s, and the gorget to protect the throat, neck and shoulders came in at the start of the 15th century. It was not until the mid-15th century that princes and great lords – the elite among knights – were riding to battle wearing complete suits of plate armour of the kind we may associate with medieval knights

▲ *From top left: the coif, made of chain mail covering the shoulders as well as the head, the chain mail tunic, and the Aketon, a quilted jacket worn beneath armour.*

through depictions in Victorian paintings. The best plate armour was made in Italy and Germany, especially at the Missaglia workshop in Milan. It was made from heat-treated steel, and at vulnerable spots between the main plates were protective roundels – or sometimes pieces of mail were worn beneath the suit.

Armour suits were highly prized, and it was accepted practice for a captured knight to give up his armour as part of his ransom. Froissart reports in his *Chronicles* that at Tournai in 1339, Pope Clement's nephew Raymond was killed after he had surrendered, slain for no better reason than that his captors coveted his beautiful armour – and this unchivalrous act 'drove many good men to anger'. The very best plate armour was superbly well made. Its chief purpose was as protection, but almost as important was its function as a status symbol – a badge of knightly pre-eminence. Plate armour was also remarkably light – hardly any heavier than chain mail. Some of the finest suits weighed as little as 25kg (55lb).

HELMETS AND SHIELDS

The simple conical helmet worn by the Normans at Hastings was gradually developed to protect the head more and more.

▼ *By the 14th century the many pieces of plate provided good protection, although the lack of a breastplate and gorget (neck piece) left knights vulnerable to the bowmen.*

▲ *Horse protection in the 1200s was made of cloth, but horse armour, first of boiled leather and then of plate metal, was developed in the course of the 15th century.*

At first soldiers wore a chain mail coif, or hood, with a padded cap beneath, then in the early 13th century they added a cylindrical helmet with a flat upper surface, a slit at eye level and tiny holes in front of nose and mouth to allow for breathing. Curved helmets were in use by *c.*1270 as experience had shown that a curved upper surface deflected blows better than a flat one. The first helmets with moveable visors were introduced at around the same time. In the 14th century pointed Italian helmets called bascinets became popular – they had a projecting 'snout' covering the mouth and were popularly known as 'hounskulls' (hounds' skulls) or 'pig-faces'.

The long kite-shaped shields carried by Normans were also used by the crusader knights. These shields generally had a

▶ *Open-face helmets were superseded first by flat-topped helmets with eye-slits, then by curved-topped ones, then by helmets with hinged visors.*

rounded top, and were made of wood covered in leather boiled until it was very hard. During the 12th century shields were made with a flatter top. As armour improved the shield was made smaller, and by the 14th century knights carried a compact arm-shield in the shape of a flat-iron known as a 'heater-shield'. By the 15th century, knights in full plate armour no longer needed to carry a shield at all, but shields were still used in tournaments.

A KNIGHT'S ROLE IN BATTLE

HOW KNIGHTS WERE DEPLOYED

The basic pattern of all battles during the age of chivalry was the same: the cavalry attacked in waves, while the infantry was primarily arrayed as a defensive block. If an attack went well, infantry poured forward to support the cavalry.

Knights were usually organized in groups of 30 to 40 fighting beneath a banner. These groups were called *conrois* and several together formed a 'battle', and two or three 'battles' might enter the conflict at once. If a feigned retreat was planned, a further battle would be held in reserve to attack unexpectedly once the enemy had broken out of his defensive position in pursuit of the retreating force.

THE NEED FOR DISCIPLINE

If the cavalry charged too soon, this could spell disaster. Leading knights were sometimes deluded by over-confidence or driven by an intense desire to achieve individual feats of glory: they led attacks

▼ *Christian forces crushed the Almohad army at the Battle of Las Navas de Tolosa in 1212. The battle was fought as part of a crusade called by Pope Innocent III.*

against impossible odds, disregarding the better judgement of more cautious fellow knights. In 1187 at the Battle of Cresson near Nazareth – shortly before the Christians' devastating defeat by Saladin at the Horns of Hattin – Templar knight Gerard of Ridefort led a mere 100 knights in a charge against a large Muslim force. Only three of the knights survived, one of whom was the architect of the disaster, Gerard himself.

Even if a cavalry charge were not against impossible odds it could still spell disaster if it were badly timed. In battlefield conditions it could be very difficult for a group of knights to reform and charge a second time. In the confused mêlée of fighting, an individual knight would have to look for the banner under which he was fighting, and might have to fight his way back to it. Effectively, the charge needed to succeed the first time.

VICTORY – OR DISASTER

Battles could be won quickly with a well-timed charge, but a position of strength could also be thrown away by impulsive knights. If the defending army weathered

the charge, it could launch its own counter-attack, often to devastating effect. It could be difficult for military commanders to maintain discipline within an army containing many proud lords and separate groups in order to prevent this kind of thing happening. For example, on crusades the knightly brotherhoods often competed for the greatest glory.

BATTLEFIELD STANDOFF

Where discipline was maintained, armies sometimes showed great reluctance to make the first move. In Spain in 1212 at the Battle of Las Navas de Tolosa the combined armies of the Christian kings of Castile, Aragon, Navarre and Portugal were arrayed for two full days in opposition to the vast force of the Muslim Almohads before fighting began. These battles often started with preliminary skirmishes between individuals or small groups who rode forward between the two armies, taunting the enemy and trying to tempt a charge. In this case Almohad warriors did just that, trying to goad the Christians into an angry response. But the Christians held firm. The attack when it came was crushingly effective, resulting in a Christian victory that killed or took prisoner 100,000 opponents.

THE EFFECT OF ARMOUR

The development of armour – from mail hauberks and byrnies to full plate armour in the 14th–15th centuries – necessarily had an effect on how knights fought. Different kinds of armour allowed for greater or lesser freedom of movement. It is a common misconception that after the development of plate armour, knights were virtually immobilized by heavy suits of armour and had to be lifted into their saddles using a small crane. In fact the armour was light and they could run and jump on to their horse wearing this equipment. Yet it is true that plate armour in both this final and its various earlier developments did tend to limit the effectiveness of a dismounted knight on the field of battle – he could not move about as easily as his predecessors had in a byrnie, simply because the plate armour was designed to be worn by a mounted warrior and not one fighting on the ground.

KNIGHTS ON FOOT

If a knight in armour were knocked from his horse, he often struggled to regain his mount, and was forced to fight on foot, when he was at a disadvantage. In the Battle of Bouvines, both Philip IV and Otto IV were unhorsed in the close fighting: Otto was saved by the bravery of his Saxon guard, but Philip – who was young and fit – managed to regain his mount and fight on. At the Battle of Poitiers in 1356, many French knights had their horses killed beneath them by English archers and were forced to try to cope on foot – with little success.

A footsoldier could quite easily bring a knight down by stabbing with his dagger through any gaps in the armour or

▼ *At the Battle of Bouvines in 1214, French cavalry power won the day in direct and bruising confrontations with the German-Flemish knights of Otto IV's army.*

at the joints between armour pieces. In the mid-14th century, at the time of the Battle of Poitiers, plate armour was gradually being developed and many knights wore both chain mail and plate armour in this period. This double armour weighed heavily upon them, and thus they were very severely handicapped once they had been unhorsed.

▲ *In many battles of the Hundred Years War, knights chose to dismount and fight alongside infantrymen. It was crucial for these footsoldiers to hold the line and turn back a cavalry charge. Knights also fought on foot after being knocked from the saddle.*

THE INFANTRY'S EFFECTIVENESS

In most battles the infantry held the key. The knights in a cavalry charge hoped to scatter the footsoldiers they rode towards, or at least to kill enough of them to break the infantry's unity as a defensive formation. If the infantry were broken up into twos and threes, then the knights could pick them off, but if the footsoldiers were able to maintain their discipline, there was little the attacking cavalry could do to best them – once knight and horse were fighting at close quarters with a solid formation of footsoldiers they were quite vulnerable. At the Battle of Hastings in 1066, the initial Norman cavalry charges had little effect and the Anglo-Saxon footsoldiers, fighting behind a wall of shields, might have carried the day had they held firm rather than breaking out to follow the feigned Norman retreat.

COEUR DE LION
KING RICHARD I OF ENGLAND

King Richard I of England is one of the most celebrated figures in the history of knighthood, hailed as Richard Coeur de Lion ('the Lionheart') for his exploits on the Third Crusade of 1190–92 when he defeated and then wisely negotiated with the great Muslim military leader Saladin. Richard was a superb general who repeatedly took the correct strategic decisions rather than clouding his judgement by a thirst for glory. Yet, like many leading figures of the era, he often did not live according to the code of chivalric honour or the doctrines of Christianity. His actions were often self-seeking and disreputable – he took part in looting, was accused of rape and suspected of murder, and rebelled twice against his own father.

▼ *This statue of Richard I outside England's Houses of Parliament perfectly depicts his heroic status in the English psyche.*

RICHARD I

Born: 8 September 1157
Died: 6 April 1199
Knighted: 1173
Famous for: his charisma, bravery in battle and his ability as a general
Greatest achievement: Defeat of Saladin, Arsuf, 7 September 1191

A TASTE FOR CHIVALRY

Born in Beaumont Palace, Oxford, in 1157, the son of King Henry II and his queen, Eleanor of Aquitaine, Richard evidently had a good education. His mother's influence was strong. She had travelled on the Second Crusade (1147–49) with her first husband, King Louis VII of France, and was a keen patroness of chivalric literature. Richard followed his mother on this path: as well as taking the Cross as a crusader, he was a major patron of poets; he himself wrote poetry in French and Occitan (a French dialect used in romances); and, according to Muslim sources, he had an interest in Arabic culture. By repute, he was a handsome man: tall, with reddish-blond hair and pale skin. He was universally praised for his bravery.

FIRST TASTE OF WAR

Richard's loyalty and sense of responsibility were certainly poorly developed. In 1173, encouraged by his mother, he joined his brothers Henry the Young King and Geoffrey, Count of Brittany, in a revolt against his father, King Henry II. The three sons gathered at the court of Eleanor's first husband, Louis VII of France. At this time, Richard was knighted by Louis, at the age of 15, and then in July 1173 rode out on his first military campaign, an invasion of eastern Normandy. The revolt failed: Henry II succeeded in imposing his authority and in 1174 Richard begged pardon and swore an oath of subservience.

▲ *Richard was a very effective leader. When he landed at Acre on the Third Crusade in April 1191, the town had been besieged for 20 months. He captured it in five weeks.*

A BRILLIANT STRATEGIST

In this period of his life Richard was duke of Aquitaine and count of Poitou, both in France. He quickly proved himself to be an outstanding warrior and general in putting down revolts by the barons in Aquitaine. The troubadour Bertran de Born wrote of the young count, 'he lays sieges and pursues his enemies, seizing their castles, smashing and burning in all directions'.

A particular example of Richard's ruthless and effective military strategy came when he took the castle of Taillebourg, near the river Charente, which was considered impregnable because it had cliff-faces around it on three sides and a town laid out on the other. He ravaged the town, farms and landscape all about, terrifying the garrison into risking all by coming out to confront him. In open battle he defeated them, and entered the castle, which he destroyed. He was merciless in wiping out the challenge of

▶ *In the Holy Land, Richard came face to face with the other great chivalric figure of his age – the Muslim general Saladin. In 1191 Richard won a great victory at Arsuf. They agreed peace terms at Jaffa in 1192.*

the barons, according to some accounts even taking their wives and forcing them to serve as prostitutes for his leading knights and then afterwards for the army.

CRUSADER KING

In 1187 Richard allied himself with Philip II of France, and then the following year again revolted against Henry II. Richard and Philip defeated Henry's forces, and Henry named his son his heir before dying. Richard was crowned King of England in Westminster Abbey on 3 September 1189 and at once set about raising money for a crusade. In 1190 he departed on crusade with Philip II.

Richard's first act on crusade was to help capture the port of Acre in June 1191. He was very ill with scurvy and laid out on a stretcher, but is said to have been strong enough to shoot down the guards on the city walls one by one using a crossbow, while his retainers carried the stretcher here and there. The garrison surrendered. Meanwhile, Philip II abandoned the crusade he had started with Richard.

After Acre Richard marched his army south towards Jaffa. Saladin launched a major attack at Arsuf, but Richard inflicted a famous defeat on the great Muslim general. Later he might have marched on Jerusalem, but seeing that he would not be able to hold the city even if he were to succeed in taking it, instead opened peace negotiations. This decision is typical of Richard's practical realism as a military commander. He agreed a treaty with

Saladin under which Jerusalem remained in Muslim hands but pilgrims could have access to it, and embarked for Europe in September 1192.

His homecoming was humiliating. He was shipwrecked, captured, imprisoned by Holy Roman Emperor Henry VI and ransomed for 150,000 marks.

DEATH AT CHALUS

After a brief visit to England in April 1194, when he was crowned king for a second time, he spent the final five years of his life fighting over his French possessions. He died after he was shot in the neck with a crossbow bolt at the castle of Chalus and the wound became gangrenous.

REPUTATION AND CHARACTER

Contemporary accounts suggest that as well as being an intelligent strategist, Richard was a charismatic commander,

beloved of his men. He repeatedly showed his bravery in combat and once rode into great danger to rescue a foraging party, with the words: 'I despatched those men there. If they die without me, then I should never again be called king.' According to the 12th-century chronicler Richard of Devizes, King Richard's men were willing to 'wade in blood to the Pillars of Hercules' at his command.

In the 20th century the idea developed that Richard was homosexual: he spent very little time with his wife, and had no children by her – although he had an illegitimate son. Some historians suggest he had a love affair with Philip II, and that this explains the ferocity of their quarrels, and it has been proposed that his wife's brother (later Sancho VII of Navarre) was another of Richard's lovers. Modern historians cast doubt on these arguments – which they say were based on a misreading of texts – and suggest that there is insufficient evidence to make conclusions about his sexuality one way or another.

◀ *Richard was buried beside his father Henry II and mother Eleanor of Aquitaine at Fontrevault Abbey near Chinon. His brain was interred separately, at Rouen.*

THE SPECTACLE OF WAR

PAGEANTRY ON THE BATTLEFIELD

Armies arrayed on a battlefield in the age of chivalry made a stirring sight. Infantry probably impressed mostly by their solid mass, and sometimes their large numbers gathered beneath fluttering banners, but the knights were an imposing sight, in helmet and armour and surcoat, mounted on powerful horses, with a colourful shield bearing a coat of arms or other armorial badge, and sword and lance and other weapons glinting in the light. In chivalric literature and in chronicles – from which we glean so much of our knowledge about how knights saw themselves and understood their calling – a knight's physical appearance was an integral part of the impact he made.

CHIVALRIC DISPLAY

Display was all-important for a knight. His armour's chief purpose was of course protection, but almost as important was its function as a status symbol – the uniform of an elite. In battle, knights were also parading their wealth and seeking to win a glorious reputation – just as they did in the mêlée conflict or individual jousts at a tournament.

▼ *Royal or noble members of the chivalric class used fine equipment as a symbol of status. Some even wore golden armour.*

In the pages of medieval epics, romances and chronicles, battles were presented as being scarcely distinguishable from tournaments – as opportunities for display and knightly encounters. The accounts are full of the glorious spectacle of knighthood in action.

ARMOUR BURNING LIKE FIRE

In the 87th *laisse* or verse-paragraph of the epic *Song of Roland*, for instance, the poet describes the army of Charlemagne as it rides through the Pass of Roncesvalles in the Pyrenees mountains. He reports that the evening sun was reflecting from their armour, so that their helmets and hauberks seemed to be made of fire, while their bright shields, painted with flowers, and their bannerets and pennons, fluttering in the breeze, made a gorgeous vision. Likewise, the Muslim army of King Marsiliun, which sweeps down to engulf Charlemagne's rearguard and kill Roland, is said to present a wondrous sight – the warriors wore golden helmets set with jewels and mail coats varnished with gilt, and carried gleaming shields. Similarly, Froissart in his *Chronicles*, describing

▲ *Italian adventurer Roger de Flor parades into Constantinople with a splendidly attired army of Almogavar Spanish mercenaries – the 'Catalan Company' – to fight for Byzantine Emperor Andronicus II Palaeologus against the Ottoman Turks.*

knights and their squires progressing forward, spear in hand, at Noya in Spain in 1387, declares: 'To tell the truth, this was a beautiful sight'.

In battle, chivalric display – wearing the finest armour, using magnificent weapons, and demonstrating great skill in using them – was a way to intimidate the enemy. According to some chronicle accounts of the Battle of Hastings, before the fighting began one of Duke William's knights rode out between the two armies to display his prowess – as a taunting expression of Norman superiority. The knight, a minstrel named Ivo Taillefer, sang a version of the *Song of Roland* while throwing his lance and sword in the air and catching them. An Anglo-Saxon warrior came forth to fight, but Taillefer killed and decapitated him – and paraded the head as proof that God was on the side of the Normans.

THE KNIGHT'S SWORD

The finest weapons were also a sign of chivalric grandeur. The sword, indeed, was the symbol of the knight's calling. In romance literature great knights had magnificent swords, that possessed within them an element of the hero's bravery and nobility: Charlemagne had Joyeuse, his knight Roland had Durendal, King Arthur had Excalibur.

The sword was a precious item, often inlaid with silver in the blade and jewels in the hilt. It was also sacred. The most common design had a sizeable crossbar between blade and hilt so that it took the shape of the Christian cross when held point downwards; squires would pray over the sword before they were knighted and then, when they were knights, before conflict. The sword itself was often blessed during the knighting ceremony.

▶ *The sword a knight carried into battle and stained with blood was a reminder of his calling as Christ's warrior, especially when used as a crucifix during prayer.*

MASSED RANKS

Aside from the wealth on display among the fighting noblemen, another aspect stressed repeatedly in chivalric literature and chronicles is the sheer size of the spectacle. King Marsiliun's army in the *Song of Roland* is a 'vast host' divided into no fewer than 20 battle formations – this is a force that attacks in a narrow mountain pass. Similarly, various chronicle accounts of the Battle of Bouvines claim that Philip IV's army included around 60,000 French – with no fewer than 9,000 knights – while Otto IV's imperial force totalled 250,000. In reality, even though the battle was fought on a much larger scale than most clashes of the 12th and 13th centuries, Philip's army probably contained no more than 1,200 knights and about 5,000 infantry, while Otto's forces had around 1,500 knights and 6,000 footsoldiers.

USE OF BANNERS

Among the colourful elements on the battlefield were the banners raised above the fighting men. They served a very necessary purpose as a rallying point for knights dispersed after a cavalry charge or by close fighting. These knights often had to fight their way back to their own banner, and it must have been very difficult for a group to reform once they were dispersed. Although military brotherhoods were in competition for glory on the field of battle, the rule of the Knights Templar laid down that if a Templar were cut off from his own banner he should seek out that of the Knights Hospitaller, or failing that any other Christian banner.

▼ *Banners flutter above the mêlée of knights and infantrymen as the English and French armies clash at the Battle of Poitiers on 9 September 1356. Edward the Black Prince led the English to a great victory.*

THE AGE OF SIEGE WARFARE
THE TECHNIQUES USED TO CAPTURE A CASTLE

In early medieval warfare the possession of castles usually provided the key to victory. Military campaigns often entailed a series of sieges. These could last for months at a time, and the fighting when it broke out was often dirty and desperate.

LOCAL STRONGHOLDS
The Normans built castles when invading, initially as a base from which to operate in subduing the territory. Once the land was conquered they used the castle as a consolidating position: its presence dominated the surrounding countryside, intimidating local people. Moreover, if an enemy approached, the castle garrison would not only stoutly defend the fortification but could venture forth from safety to harass the enemy with raids.

For this reason an army could not safely bypass a castle and move on to a more distant target because that would leave its rear and its supply lines wide open to raids from the castle garrison. An invading army had to capture castles, either eliminating or forcing the surrender of the garrison before moving on.

ATTACK OR SIEGE
Castles were designed to withstand attack. An attacking army had two main options: to launch an assault quickly or to mount a siege, cut off supplies and reduce the garrison to desperation.

There were several difficulties with mounting a siege. In a prolonged siege, it could be difficult to hold the besieging army together – feudal levies might come to an end of their period of service and depart for home. It is noticeable that King Henry II of England, who mounted many successful sieges, used mercenary troops who were happy to remain and be paid, however long the siege went on. There was also the risk of sickness setting in amongst the besiegers, as happened to the crusaders at Acre in 1189–91.

Moreover, a well-sited castle could be well-nigh impossible to isolate totally – for example, King Edward I of England established his formidable Welsh castles so that they could be supplied by sea. It was due to this that in the Welsh rebellion led by Madoc ap Llywelyn in 1294 none of the rebels' sieges of the castles was successful.

In 1401, by contrast, Owain Glyndwr, self-styled 'Prince of Wales', succeeded in taking Harlech Castle after a siege because he was able to mount a total blockade – by his own troops on land and by a fleet supplied by his French allies at sea.

SIEGE EQUIPMENT
Attackers often used specialist siege equipment to try to make a hole in the castle defences – machines such as the mangonel and trebuchet, which hurled stones at the walls of the castle. They sometimes used battering rams to try to knock the walls down; at others they tried to scale the walls using ladders – a technique known as escalade. This was highly dangerous since as they mounted, the attackers were liable to be wounded or killed by arrows, missiles or liquids sent their way by members of the garrison on the castle walls.

▼ *The concentric fortifications of Harlech Castle in Wales stand atop a 60m (200ft) rock. The English garrison survived a major siege by the forces of Madoc ap Llywelyn during the Welsh revolt of 1294–95.*

A better technique was to use a belfry, a tall tower that was set up against the besieged castle's walls. The belfry was usually built taller than the defensive walls so that the attackers could climb to the top, then fire down on the garrison before clambering over the walls along a bridge lowered from the belfry top. The belfry was usually made of wood, but covered in water-drenched animal skins to make it harder for the defenders to set fire to it as a way of repelling the assault.

The tactics used to break the spirit of a defending garrison were often highly unchivalrous. For example, King Henry V of England captured Rouen, France, in 1418–19 because he had cut off its water supplies and thrown dead animals into the accessible wells. Eventually a plague broke out in the city and the garrison was forced to surrender.

THE ROLE OF KNIGHTS

Knights did not frequently play much of a role in the initial stages of a siege. Specialist soldiers usually operated the siege equipment such as the mangonel, trebuchet or battering ram. Knights would then lead an assault, clambering up the belfry or pouring through a breach in the

▲ English troops fire from a siege tower and pour over a ladder into a French town in the Hundred Years War. On the walls the defenders put up a desperate resistance.

▼ Three crusader armies – those of the kingdom of Jerusalem (upper left), of France (lower left) and of Germany (right) combine at the Siege of Damascus during the Second Crusade. The abject failure of their attack brought the crusade to an end.

walls once one was made. On the other side knights were often members of the besieged castle garrison, so once battle was joined over or through the walls chivalric encounters did occur between the two groups of knights.

FIGHTING IN A MINE

Another means of attack was to try to make the walls collapse by digging beneath them. The attackers would dig a mine; within, the defenders would dig a counter-mine in order to repel them. The defenders would place a bowl of water on the ground at various points within the outer walls and if they saw ripples on the water this indicated that digging was going on underground and that a mine was nearby. Where two mines met, it was – rather strangely – the custom for knights on opposing sides to meet in individual combat in the mines. In the autumn of 1420, during his siege of the town of Melun in France, King Henry V of England took part in mounted combat in a mine dug beneath the town walls that was lit by torches along the walls of the mine. These encounters were a good opportunity for acts of high chivalry, and it was the custom for the knights who fought in them to become lifelong chivalric associates – 'brothers in arms'.

PILLAGING AND BURNING
THE REALITY OF MEDIEVAL WARFARE

Many medieval campaigns featured the ravaging of countryside and cities, particularly in the mid-14th century during the Hundred Years War between England and France. These pillaging raids were known as *chevauchée* (from the French term for a 'charge of horses', presumably because the small raiding army moved at great speed across the countryside). The raids were planned as a form of economic warfare to undermine the enemy's capacity to continue the fight by attacking their supplies and resources. Moreover, in an age when the leading generals were often reluctant to risk their infantry and knights in a pitched fight on the field of battle, chevauchée raiding was designed to force a defending army to leave the relative safety of a beseiged castle or a fortified town, and to come out to fight in the field.

▼ *When an invading army swept across the countryside, setting homes and farms ablaze, frightened locals were powerless to stand in its way.*

THE PILLAGING OF NORMANDY
In July 1346 King Edward III of England and his son Edward Prince of Wales (later known as 'the Black Prince') landed in Normandy and marched their army along the Contentin Peninsula and westwards to Caen, raiding and pillaging as they went.

▲ *Generals, leading knights and even lesser members of an army could grow rich on the wealth that they looted from captured cities and towns.*

With support from an English fleet out at sea, Edward mounted a swift and brutal attack on Caen. His soldiers poured through the streets, taking their pleasure and plundering the city's wealth. If the chronicle reports that Edward had banned maltreatment of women, children and religious houses are to be believed, then the ban was disregarded during the brutal sacking of the city.

Caen was a scene of devastation and rapine. Chronicler Jean Froissart, as always emphasizing chivalric deeds by great knights, reported in his *Chronicles* that Sir Thomas Holland rode through the town, and managed to save the lives of many women, children, nuns and monks from the maddened English mob. The booty was loaded on to the ships of the fleet to be taken back across the Channel – Froissart notes that the ships were 'weighed down with fine clothes, precious jewels, and silver or gold objects'.

SCORCHED EARTH

Chevauchée warfare resulted not only in looting but in wanton destruction and the burning of great swathes of countryside. In 1339 during an early campaign using the chevauchée tactic led by Edward III, a chronicler climbed at night to the top of a church tower in the vicinity of Cambrai, northern France, and saw the countryside ablaze in all directions for many miles around – a vision of hell risen to the earth's surface.

The raids deliberately undermined the capacity of the enemy to fight back by depriving him of resources and support. In 1355–57 Edward the Black Prince led a chevauchée campaign in France specifically designed to hit towns that were strong financial supporters of the French monarchy. Sir John Wingfield, the Black Prince's steward and councillor, wrote that the lands and towns destroyed in the raids 'found for the king of France each year more to maintain his war than did half his kingdom'.

POLITICAL CHALLENGE

If an English army raided with apparent impunity in France it was a demonstration of the power of the English crown, and a calculated insult to the king of France. In the summer of 1370 Sir Robert Knowles (or Knollys) marched unchallenged from Calais to the Île de France (Paris), laying waste the countryside en route, and then taunting the French king in his capital city.

The raids were designed to undermine the French monarch's support among his citizens in the ravaged area. When the local people saw that royal protection counted for nothing, they would lose faith in their king. Often, indeed, the raids forced the enemy to launch reprisals.

Both of the chevauchée campaigns that were conducted by Edward, the Black Prince, in 1346 and 1355–57, drew a military response from the French in the field – they resulted in the celebrated English victories at the Battle of Crécy (1346) and Poitiers (1356). Indeed, this was a principal part of their purpose, for the

English – with their widely feared archers – were confident of victory in the pitched battles that occurred during the Hundred Years War.

ECONOMICAL WARFARE

Chevauchée was extremely profitable because it resulted in the capture of mounds of booty and hundreds of ransomed prisoners. Moreover, it was an economical way to wage war because the raids could be carried out by small armies of a few thousand men and did not call for the expense of long campaigns involving major battles or prolonged sieges. The raids delivered effective blows to the enemy's finances and morale but did not result in conquests that had to be defended with permanent and expensive garrisons.

THE BRUTALITY OF WILLIAM I

Chevauchée is particularly associated by historians with the mid-14th century campaigns in the Hundred Years' War, but

▲ *Women and children, as well as defenders, faced a dreadful fate when a fortified town fell to its besiegers. Army commanders would often turn a blind eye to the activities of their looting soldiers.*

punitive raiding was certainly used elsewhere as an aspect of military policy. For example, William I used similar tactics in his infamous 'Harrying of the North' in 1069–70, when his army burned villages, destroyed the crops and livestock, and devastated the populations across much of northern England. He is reckoned to have killed 150,000 people, with more succumbing to starvation and plague in the course of the long winter that followed in a ravaged landscape. The crusaders also made use of the tactic in the Holy Land. It was also adopted during the raiding in the mid-14th century across the English–Scottish border, when both English and Scots used merciless violence in ravaging the countryside.

THE BLACK DOUGLAS

SIR JAMES DOUGLAS, LORD OF DOUGLAS

Sir James Douglas, a great knight in the Scottish wars of independence in the early 14th century, was a brilliant exponent of guerrilla warfare, a man whose violent raids on English castles and towns in the Scottish borders won him the affection of his countrymen and the hatred of his English enemies – the Scots knew him as 'Good Sir James', while the English called him 'the Black Douglas'. He was a close battle companion of Robert the Bruce (King Robert I of Scots). He died fighting against the Saracens in Spain en route to the Holy Land, where he had promised to bury Robert the Bruce's embalmed heart.

SQUIRE IN PARIS

Sir James's father was Sir William Douglas the Hardy (also 'the Bold'), who was Governor of Berwick Castle when it was brutally sacked by the army of King Edward I of England on Good Friday 1296. Sir William was subsequently freed, and supported the Scots freedom fighter Sir William Wallace, but was recaptured and died in captivity in 1298 in the Tower of London. In this period the youthful James Douglas was in Paris, where he had been sent by his family to be safe, and where he entered the service of William Lamberton, Bishop of St Andrews, as a squire. When he returned to Scotland in 1306 with Bishop William, Douglas found that his family estates had been taken and given to one of Edward I's loyal soldiers, Robert de Clifford.

Bishop William introduced Douglas at the English court, but when Edward refused to contemplate restoring the family estates to the young man, Douglas allied himself with Robert the Bruce, who had claimed the Scottish crown after killing his principal rival John Comyn. It was during these years that Douglas learned the guerrilla warfare that he would put to such devastating use.

▲ *At Bannockburn in 1314, Sir James – on the very day of his knighting – commanded one of the four divisions of the 6,500-strong Scottish army of Robert the Bruce.*

THE 'DOUGLAS LARDER'

On Palm Sunday, 19 March 1307, Douglas led a brutal assault on the English garrison in Douglas Castle, the stronghold that should rightfully have been his own possession. He and his troops surprised the garrison celebrating the holy day, breaking into the church with the battle-cry 'Douglas! Douglas!' and slaying many there and then. Afterwards he beheaded the surviving garrison members, and cast their corpses atop a great fire that he had built from wine casks taken from the castle cellar. He poisoned the wells by throwing dead horses and salt into them. The attack was known as 'the Douglas larder'.

He struck again to capture the English-held Roxburgh Castle in 1314. He ordered his men to approach the castle in the dark on the night of Shrove Tuesday, crawling beneath their cloaks – when the guards looked out from the battlements in the darkness they thought the dark shapes were nothing more threatening than wandering cattle. Suddenly the Scots soldiers threw hooked scaling ladders up the walls, and poured into the castle, surprising the garrison – who were distracted by their pre-Lenten celebrations. He then slighted the castle (damaged its defences so that it was indefensible by the garrison).

A KNIGHT AT BANNOCKBURN

Later that year Douglas fought alongside the Bruce in the Scots' famous victory at Bannockburn over a much larger English army. On the morning of the battle, 24 June, Douglas was knighted – surprisingly late in life, given his many great military exploits, but an interesting example of how many men fought on as squires for several years.

It was in the years after Bannockburn that Douglas won his reputation as 'the Black Douglas' through his relentless raiding of northern England. On these raids he and his men rode on ponies called 'hobbins' and dismounted to fight on foot – soldier and horse together were called 'hobelars'. Douglas defeated many notable

---

> **JAMES DOUGLAS**
> **Born**: 1286
> **Died**: 25 August 1330
> **Knighted**: 24 June 1314
> **Famous for**: his lightning raids on northern England
> **Greatest achievement**: defeat of Sir Robert Neville of Middleham, 1318

---

opponents in these conflicts including Sir Robert Neville of Middleham, known as 'the Peacock of the North'.

'DOUGLAS! DOUGLAS!'

In April 1318 Douglas took part in the capture of Berwick Castle, then England's last notable possession in Scotland. Edward II of England rode north with an army to take it back, bringing his queen, Isabella, with him as far as York. In 1319, with the English army encamped outside Berwick, Douglas led a raid into Yorkshire, forcing Isabella to flee southwards, and defeated an English army raised by the Archbishop of York that mainly consisted of clergy, in the Battle of Myton.

Douglas continued to be a thorn in the side of the English. In 1327 when the teenage King Edward III led an army northwards, Douglas launched a night raid on their camp at Stanhope in northern England, his men roaring through the camp with the terrifying shout of 'Douglas! Douglas!', killing 300 Englishmen and almost taking the king himself prisoner.

DEATH IN SPAIN

King Robert the Bruce died in 1329, but before he died he asked Sir James, by now his oldest companion in arms, to take his heart to the Holy Sepulchre in Jerusalem. Sir James set out in 1330, with the dead king's embalmed heart enclosed in a silver casket hung around his neck.

On the way he and his companions heard that King Alfonso XI of Castile and León had declared a crusade against the Saracens in Spain and – as good knights, being ever hungry for glory in the service

of Christ – diverted there. In a battle at Teba, Douglas went to the aid of a fellow knight surrounded by Saracens. They were badly outnumbered, but Douglas plunged into the thick of the conflict, throwing the silver casket with Bruce's heart ahead of him, and shouted 'You go ahead, as was our custom, and I will follow you – even into death!' Douglas was indeed killed and afterwards his body, and the Bruce's heart, were taken back to Scotland. Douglas was buried in St Bride's Kirk, Douglas, and the Bruce's heart was buried at Melrose Abbey.

CHIVALRY IN PRACTICE

Sir James was a celebrated knight of his day, but it cannot be said that he fought according to the laws of chivalry. His favoured method of guerrilla warfare was both necessary, given limited Scottish resources, and very effective, but it relied on subterfuge, deception and ruthlessness. His stirring life story is by no means unique in the medieval period in providing many examples of how the code of chivalry was an ideal that many knights had often to abandon in order to thrive.

▼ *An English archer leads an assault on Berwick Castle, whose position in the English and Scottish borders meant it changed hands many times. Sir James endured a siege there by the army of King Edward II in 1318–19.*

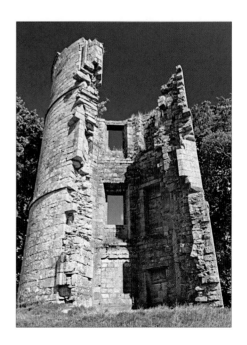

▼ *This tower is all that remains today of Douglas Castle, scene of Sir James's Easter attack on the English garrison in 1307. At that time the castle was just 19 years old, having been built in 1288.*

THE BUSINESS OF WAR
HOW KNIGHTS MADE MONEY ON CAMPAIGN AND IN TOURNAMENTS

In raiding and through the raising of ransoms, knights could acquire great wealth. While chivalry emphasized purer motives for fighting, such as seeking glory or exhibiting loyalty to a noble lord, in practice knights accepted the rewards that came their way.

RANSOMS

A knight captured in battle was ransomed, often for very large sums of money. There was a generally accepted understanding that the ransom should not be set at so high a level that the knight would be ruined, and thereafter be unable to keep maintaining himself as a knight.

A king's ransom could be vast. King Richard I of England, captured in 1192 on his way home from the Third Crusade, and imprisoned by Duke Leopold of Austria and Holy Roman Emperor Henry VI, was ransomed for 150,000 marks –

▼ *Many knights, including Bertrand du Guesclin, seen here being made High Constable of France by King Charles IV , made great fortunes through accumulating the legitimate spoils of war.*

> ### RANSOMS AND THE KNIGHTLY CODE
> Honoré Bonet, the late-14th-century Provençal prior and writer on chivalry, considered in his *Arbre des Batailles* ('Tree of Battles', 1382–87) whether the setting of ransoms was consistent with chivalric conduct and concluded that it was, declaring: 'All that a soldier can win from his opponent in lawful war he has the right to retain', adding that the act of taking ransom from a prisoner had been 'approved' by 'custom and usage'. He went on, however, to complain that many knights acted without pity or mercy in demanding excessive ransoms, and suggested that they should limit themselves to a 'reasonable and knightly' amount.

equivalent to 35 tonnes of gold, and about three times the English crown's annual income. This vast sum was raised from his English subjects by Chief Justiciar Hubert Walter through the seizing of valuable church plate and the imposition of swingeing taxes (a quarter of the value of property) on both clergy and lay people.

After King John II 'the Good' of France was captured at the Battle of Poitiers in 1356, a ransom of 3,000,000 marks was demanded. This was never paid as John was released, with his son Louis held in Calais as a hostage, in order to raise the sum, and then when Louis escaped, John voluntarily gave himself up into captivity once more.

RANSOMS AND HONOUR

A high ransom was in one sense a sign of honour. When the 'Eagle of Brittany', the great Breton knight Bertrand du Guesclin, was captured by Edward the Black Prince at the Battle of Najera (Navarrette) in Spain

▲ *Son of a Florentine merchant, Pippo Spano was a knight in the service of Sigismund, King of Hungary and Holy Roman Emperor from 1433 to 1437. Sigismund rewarded Pippo with the control of all the gold mines in Hungary.*

in April 1367, he taunted his captor saying he would not dare grant him his freedom. The Black Prince responded by telling du Guesclin to name his own ransom and he set it at the vastly inflated level of 100,000 francs – boasting that in France he was so highly regarded that even the peasant women would contribute to his ransom. In the event even this enormous payment was given by the French king.

At the other end of the scale, a poor knight might be required to raise a few crowns for his ransom. Sometimes a knight merely forfeited his armour and his horse and weapons and was allowed to go free – even this penalty was considerable, for the cost of horse and equipment was high.

NECESSARY FINANCES

Seeking land and wealth has been a motive in going to war from time immemorial. The mounted warriors of Duke William of Normandy's army at Hastings were not required to be there by feudal loyalty, for their vows of service did not extend beyond the lord's territory: they were drawn, as countless warriors before them, by the promise of the riches they could acquire through conquest. Similarly, one among the many motives for knights going on crusade was seeking riches in the Holy Land.

Throughout the age of chivalry, many lesser knights – those whose fiefs were too small to support them adequately – knew that the wealth acquired with sword and lance was necessary for their very survival. There were knights who rose from a humble beginning to positions of extraordinary power, such as the impoverished Italian knight, Pippo Spano, who became the confidant, trusted strategist and general of the King of Hungary, and as such was granted large portions of land, noble titles, and national assets such as control of Hungary's gold mines, that guaranteed him a substantial income.

In chivalric tournaments, as well as on the field of battle, and in feudal politics, knights could make a living from their martial skills – for defeated opponents in the mêlée and joust could be required to pay ransom and to surrender their horse and equipment. Battles between Christian knights in the European theatre of war,

battles in which there was limited risk of dying because the conflict was not pursued to the death, were thus in many ways highly comparable to tournaments – good opportunities for establishing a public reputation for chivalry and a private fortune.

SHARING OUT THE BOOTY

In the 14th century, when a town was formally besieged and its occupants did not take the opportunity to surrender, according to the laws of chivalry its riches were forfeit to the invaders, save that

▲ *King John II is taken captive at the Battle of Poitiers. Lords had little to fear as their ransoms ensured they were treated well.*

clergy and churches were spared. The normal custom was for spoils to be divided three ways, with the first part being divided among the soldiery and knights, the second part being reserved for the commander, and the remainder sent home to the king. Not all these sieges ended in a frenzied sacking as at Caen – often there was an ordered entry and taking of booty. A more formal system was introduced in England in the second half of the 14th century under the indentures of war. In accordance with these, the commander was required to give up to the king the most important castles, towns and prisoners and he would be rewarded for this. The remaining spoil was split, two-thirds to the commander and one-third to the crown.

◄ *A commander would reward his leading knights and soldiers out of his two-thirds share of a conquered town's spoils.*

CHIVALRY IN WARFARE

THE CODE OF CHIVALRY ON THE BATTLEFIELD

The code of chivalric behaviour laid down the boundaries of good conduct both on the battlefield and during sieges. However, in practice, fighting was often dirtier than chivalry would readily countenance. In addition, success in war depended on qualities such as discipline that were at odds with chivalry's emphasis on the pursuit of individual glory.

DEMANDS OF CHIVALRY

In battles of the age of chivalry, fighting to the death was only normal in wars against 'the infidel' – meaning those who were not Christians, principally the Islamic soldiers in the Holy Land and in Spain, or pagan fighters in the Baltic region. In conflicts such as the Hundred Years War, particularly in clashes between noble knights, it was normal to take prisoners and to ransom them at great profit.

▼ *A Breton warrior surrenders to a French knight at the Battle of Saint-Aubin-du-Cormier in 1488. In such moments of chivalry the brute energy of the medieval battlefield was suddenly stilled.*

When a town or castle was besieged, chivalry demanded that the siege be declared by a herald. Once this was done, the garrison or the townspeople could surrender at any point up to the scaling of the walls. There are numerous examples of garrisons and populations being treated with great clemency, in accordance with these rules – such as cases of fighting

▲ *When a town fell, its inhabitants were at the mercy of the victorious troops. Even within the code of chivalry, at the end of a siege soldiers could lawfully run riot.*

being suspended to allow populations who had taken refuge in a castle to exit while the garrison remained behind to carry on the fight. King Edward III of England allowed non-soldiers free exit from Calais in northern France, when he was besieging the town in 1346; he even gave them food and money. If defenders remained defiant, then when the assault finally came the soldiers of the invading army were entitled to help themselves to the riches within the walls – except that church buildings, priests, monks and nuns could not be touched.

THE SACKING OF LIMOGES

Often when a long siege came to an end the victorious besiegers ran out of control, inflicting dreadful suffering on the garrison or townsfolk. The knights of the First Crusade when entering Jerusalem in 1099 set a terrible example, slaughtering men, women and children until the streets reputedly ran with blood. As we have seen, Edward III and the Black Prince oversaw the horrific sacking of Caen in 1346, while – according to Froissart – at Limoges in 1370 the Black Prince himself took part in a savage raid on the city following the conclusion of the siege. Froissart's account of the attack on Limoges suggests that the prince was maddened with anger that his old ally, the Bishop of Limoges, had gone over to the French side – and ordered the sacking of the city in which more than 3,000 men, women and children were slaughtered.

FAILURE OF DISCIPLINE

On many occasions, it appears that knights were unable to control their men. Armies often contained a good proportion of unruly elements – not least because the English armies in France during the Hundred Years War contained criminals who had been offered a free pardon in return for volunteering for service.

Moreover, it may be that knights felt that the misbehaviour of the lower orders in the army did not reflect badly on them – that the code of chivalry principally bound the noblemen who were knights, and that it was understandable that the lower classes would be unable to live up to chivalry's high standards. This is the view put forward by Froissart when describing the devastation at Caen – that the rampaging mob was full of 'wicked fellows and doers of evil, the sort you inevitably find in a royal army'.

Yet there were also occasions on which knights could not control themselves – when they also took part in the sacking of towns and profited greatly from them; and when they did not adhere to the code of chivalry in battle, abandoning its ties in moments of rage or in the physical excitement and turmoil of the battlefield.

QUEST FOR GLORY

In one important sense self-discipline and the chivalric code were at odds. Knights were expected to seek glory; the code of chivalry demanded that they should be eager to prove again and again their knightly status through acts of martial endeavour. In battle they were ready to seize any opportunity to do this. Yet then as now, armies required discipline, and to be most effective usually needed to function as a unit. There are countless examples of knights acting rashly and against the interests of their commanders in order to seek glory for themselves or for their knightly brotherhood.

The Templar knights were often a law unto themselves in this regard. In the siege of Ascalon (Ashkelon in Israel) mounted by Baldwin III of Jerusalem in 1153, the Templars even fought against their own side in the search for glory: when a breach was made in the walls opposite the Templar quarters in the camp, a group of 40 knights led by Bernard of Tremblay went in to take the city, while others prevented non-Templars from joining. In the event, the 40 Templar knights had taken on too much, and they were defeated, captured and killed, and their heads were hung from the city walls.

During the Seventh Crusade at Al Mansourah in Egypt in 1250, the Templar Robert I, Count of Artois, led a charge of fellow members of the brotherhood despite specific orders to hold back. He surprised part of the Egyptian army but then his troops swept on into the streets of the town, where they were ambushed and he was killed; the Egyptians were able to launch a counter-offensive against the main army, which robbed the crusaders of the land they had just won.

▼ *Templar knights pour forward, despite a hail of arrows, towards their Saracen foes. The Templars and Hospitallers were an often unpredictable part of the crusade armies, liable to launch independent attacks in search of their own glory.*

CHAPTER FIVE

THE KNIGHT OF THE TOURNEY

In January 1430 Philip the Good, Duke of Burgundy, hosted a magnificent banquet followed by a six-day tournament to celebrate his marriage to Isabella, daughter of King John I of Portugal. To welcome the new duchess to Bruges he hung vermilion cloth in the streets, laid on fountains of wine and built a magnificent temporary banqueting hall containing a gilded tree hung with his heraldic arms. During the tournament two teams of knights jousted in three sets of lists built in the city's marketplace. Each day a golden chain or sparkling jewel was presented to the best knight and squire of each team. At the end of the tournament Philip announced the creation of a new chivalric order, the Order of the Golden Fleece. The duke's tournament was one of the most lavish of the entire Middle Ages, and the culmination of a long tradition of chivalric competitions. Tournaments were absolutely central to the world of medieval knights. They developed from martial manoeuvres, and throughout their history were always valued by knights as a form of military training. Crucially, also, they provided a setting for knights to display their chivalric virtues such as bravery, courtesy, humility and generosity. They were inspired by, and themselves inspired, the developing culture of chivalry and courtly love, an arena where knights competed for the approval of watching ladies. The tournament was also a place of opportunity, for knights could grow rich on the winnings.

▲ *Medieval jousts were the extravagant entertainment spectacles of the day.*

◄ *Sir Tristan and Sir Palomides fight in the lists as other knights of the Round Table look on. According to Arthurian legend, Palomides was inspired by a glimpse of the lady he adored, Iseult, to become unbeatable in the tournament – despite the fact that she loved Tristan.*

MARTIAL GAMES
THE ORIGIN OF TOURNAMENTS

A spectacle incorporating military training, tournaments have precursors going back to the classical world. In the medieval era the lavish and formal courtly entertainments of the kind held by Philip the Good developed from the rough and tumble of cross-country cavalry manoeuvres.

THE EXAMPLE OF ROME

From the time of ancient Greece and Rome, if not earlier, soldiers and their generals understood the need for martial games and manoeuvres as part of military training. The young men of Sparta and of Rome developed their strength and their soldierly prowess in mock combats. In the medieval period, knights and writers on chivalry saw tournaments as emulating the fighting contests of the classical world. Tournaments, particularly when they took the form of a pair of knights jousting in the lists, also had forerunners in classical and pre-medieval combats, such as the gladiatorial contests so popular in ancient Rome and in the trials by combat used by Germanic tribes to resolve their disputes.

▼ *Most gladiators in ancient Rome were slaves. Like a joust, gladiatorial combat was both a trial of strength and entertainment.*

FRANKISH CAVALRY MANOEUVRES

The Frankish cavalry practised riding at speed, changing direction sharply and controlling a horse among a crowd of many others. One celebrated account of these manoeuvres describes 'war games' held at Strasbourg in 842 to celebrate the alliance of Charlemagne's grandsons, Louis the German and Charles the Bald.

In the games, groups of cavalry rode fast towards each other, then one group wheeled away, protecting themselves with shields, and pretending to flee, drawing their opponents into a charge before suddenly turning and driving back the charge. Finally the kings, Louis and Charles, rode into the battle with their lances aloft, urging on the two sides. Frankish historian Nithard described the event, noting that the encounter was a great sight, partly due to the many nobles taking part and also because they were so well ordered. Some modern historians have claimed this was the first medieval tournament, although it was not a true tourney because it was not a combat – the two sides charged and fled but did not fight.

▲ *The city-state of Sparta rose to power in the 8th–5th centuries BC with an army of super-fit soldiers who fought mock battles to develop their skills – similarly, tournaments honed the prowess a knight needed for war.*

BATTLES IN OPEN COUNTRY

The first proper tournaments were probably mock battles that took place between groups of Frankish cavalry in France in the late 11th century. Two sets of knights, often from different areas, fought across open countryside. They rode across farmland and forests and took full advantage of the opportunities for ambush provided by buildings and natural features. There were often as many as 200 knights on each side, led by the same lords they followed in war. The purpose of the game was to capture and then ransom as many knights as possible from the other team.

The knights fought with real weapons including lances, bows and arrows – and injuries were common. There were no rules, save that fighting must not be to the death, and that knights could take refuge and rest in fenced-off neutral areas.

▲ When tournaments were held in the streets, onlookers ran the risk of being hurt by the galloping horses and flailing knights.

TOURNEYING ON CRUSADE

Formal tournaments developed out of these cross-country battles. The Franks probably carried the sport with them when they went on the First Crusade – the chronicler Robert the Monk noted that when not fighting they practised tilting at the quintain (riding towards a target with a couched lance). Tournaments, indeed, emerged at the time that the Franks or Normans began using the couched lance in battle, a very demanding technique that required a lot of practice – and it may well be that tournaments developed initially out of the need to practise it.

FIRST REFERENCES

The first use of the word 'tournament' is in legislation of 1114, issued by Count Baldwin III of Hainaut, which describes keepers of the peace neglecting their jobs and leaving the town of Valenciennes to partake in 'javelin games, tournaments and similar sports'. Around the same time, in *c*.1115–20, the Benedictine monk and chronicler Geoffrey of Malaterra observed that in campaigns in Sicily by his fellow Normans, the young knights tourneyed during the course of a siege in the year 1062 – this indicates that tournaments were being held in *c*.1120, when he was

writing, even if his account of 1062 is fictitious. Then in the 1140s, a history of the Church of St Martin of Tournai referred to the death of Count Henry III of Brabant in a tournament between his warriors and those of Tournai in 1095.

CREATIVE ACCOUNTS

Caution is advised when reading accounts of early tournaments since in later years a way of proving knightly heritage was to demonstrate that one's ancestors had fought in tournaments for generations; medieval chroniclers often rewrote the

past, inventing great encounters at tournaments to add lustre to the reputation of their lords. The 16th-century herald Georg Ruexner claimed in his *Book of Tournaments* (*c*.1530) that King Henry I of Germany held glamorous tournaments in 938 in Magdeburg; but certain details in his description cast doubt on his account. The chronicle of St Martin of Tours refers to the supposed origin of tournaments: it says that a nobleman named Geoffrey de Preilly, who it says was ambushed and killed at Angers in 1066, should be remembered as the inventor of the sport.

WHAT WAS A TOURNAMENT?

Strictly speaking a tournament was a mock battle between two sets of knights – the combat also known as a *mêlée*. The knights fought as units, just as in battle, with the aim of defeating the other side and so winning their opponents' equipment and horses. In France and England this was often also called a *hastilude* ('spear contest'), and it was the principal form of the tournament in England in the 13th century when Sir William Marshal rose to prominence due to his martial skills. It was a distinct

contest from jousting. However, the word 'tournament' began to be used, especially in Germany, for the courtly events that encompassed both mêlées and jousting, and it certainly has the more general meaning in modern usage.

▶ Two teams of knights from Arthur's Round Table compete as groups in the form of the tournament known as a hastilude.

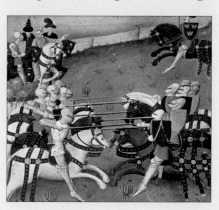

PROWESS ON DISPLAY

TYPES OF TOURNAMENT

The 12th-century English chronicler Roger of Hoveden defined tournaments as 'military exercises performed not in a hostile spirit but only to practise and put prowess on display'. Across the centuries of the chivalric period, the tournament took a number of forms – most, in line with Roger's definition, devoted to the sport of mounted contests, but some much closer to actual warfare.

THE MÊLÉE

The earliest formal tournaments seem to have taken the form of mock battles of the kind fought by the Franks in the fields of northern France, but in an enclosed area rather than in open country. In this type

▼ *Knights take an oath before participating in the tournament. The competitors are split into two 'teams' to fight in the mêlée.*

of encounter, called a mêlée, two teams of knights fought with couched lances.

The two groups represented home and away teams – the 'defenders' (those associated with the town or region in which the tournament was being held) and the 'attackers' (visitors from elsewhere). The two sides first paraded into position and called out their cries of war, then rested briefly while in the land between the two sides young knights charged at one another in individual jousts.

At a signal the main charge began: the two groups headed for one another with couched lances, then turned swiftly to fight individually or in small groups. The word 'tournament' is believed to derive from the French *tournement* ('turning'), a reference to the quick reversal of direction. Squires stood by to offer up to three replacement lances to their lords.

From an account in Wolfram von Eschenbach's great 13th-century poem *Parzifal* we learn that a knight in one of these charges aimed for his opponent to the left and carried his couched lance across the neck of his mount, aiming at his rival's shield. After the charge, the mêlée often spread out beyond the original lists into a designated area of countryside or even into the streets of the town as knights carried on the fight, trying to take as many of their opponents captive as possible.

THE JOUST

The mêlée was quite dangerous and often resulted in serious injury or death. Over time it became less common and tournaments primarily featured jousting between two knights. In a joust the knights rode towards one another with couched lance, each aiming to unhorse his opponent.

From about 1400, in an attempt to limit injuries, the knights rode either side of a central barrier called the tilt. Probably developed in Spain or Portugal, the tilt spread throughout Europe during the 15th century; it was already common in France by 1430. At first it seems to have been no more than a cloth hanging from a rope, but quickly this became a stout wooden barrier with padding.

In the 11th–12th centuries individual jousting was often a sideshow to the main event, which was the mêlée. Jousting might take place on the eve of the tournament or on the morning of the contest, prior to the main combat. The 13th and 14th centuries saw jousting becoming more popular, and some tournaments featured only individual combat with lances.

Although the conditions of the mêlée provided better practice for battle than did a joust, knights tended to prefer jousting because their individual prowess was more obvious in individual combat. Jousting certainly had its dangers but it was generally safer than the mêlée, with less danger of the horses trampling unseated riders.

THE BOHORT

Less formal contests between mounted knights continued to be held alongside tournaments. One of these was the *béhouard*, also known as the *buhurt* (in 12th-century German) or, in English, the bohort. This was more sport than conflict, an encounter between knights relying principally on their horsemanship, and using weapons less than in a tournament. For this reason, while the tournament was often condemned by state and Church authorities, the bohort was viewed more kindly. The rules of the Knights Templar stated that brothers must not compete in tournaments but were allowed to take part in bohorts. Sometimes bohorts were enacted by squires rather than knights.

Bohorts were described often in chivalric literature, where they were the natural conclusion to a wedding or knighting ceremony. In Geoffrey of Monmouth's *History of the Kings of Britain*, King Arthur's knights

are described as riding out to hold an impromptu bohort after feasting at one of the king's courts: and while the ladies cheered from the town walls, the knights sported in the meadows, riding and throwing lances and competing with bows and arrows. Geoffrey emphasizes that the competition was only for sport, and never in earnest, and that it did not provoke the smallest display of bad feeling.

PRACTICE MEETINGS

New knights needed practice before they entered the very demanding mêlée arena and the jousting lists. Practice sessions called vespers were often laid on for the inexperienced on the eve of major tournaments, but sometimes entire contests were held specifically to give the young knights practice. In Germany this type of tournament was called the *tirocinium*.

PAS D'ARMES AND CHALLENGES TO ARMS

In the late 14th and 15th centuries very lavish tournaments called *pas d'armes* ('passage of arms') were held. These were so magnificent in conception and presentation that only kings, princes and leading nobles could afford to mount them. Examples include the tournament held by Philip the Good in 1430.

▲ Jousts were often fought until a specified number of lances had been broken. In this tournament, fought in the reign of King Charles V of France (1338–80), broken lances litter the ground in the lists.

Poorer knights, who could not afford to organize a *pas d'armes*, arranged their own chivalric contests by issuing 'challenges to arms'. A good example is the open challenge issued by seven knights of France in 1398 to any seven knights from England. The French knights agreed to wear a diamond on their armour for three years and to be ready to fight on challenge by an English knight, with lance, then sword, then axe, then dagger. Should the English knight win, he could keep the diamond, but should he lose he would be required to supply seven golden rods, one for each of the French victors, for them to pass on to their devoted ladies. We have no record of the result of this challenge.

Four French knights travelled to Parliament in London to issue a challenge for jousts at Calais, and the king granted licences to English knights to respond. Another example is the celebrated Joust of St Inglevert in northern France in 1390, when four knights proclaimed that they would occupy the lists for a period of 30 days and fight all comers.

HERALDS AND CHALLENGES
WHEN AND HOW TOURNAMENTS WERE HELD

Tournaments were often held to add pageantry and colour to great royal or noble state occasions. These entertainments needed careful organization.

COURTLY CELEBRATIONS

At royal and noble courts tournaments were associated, first and foremost, with weddings. The chivalric Edward I held a tournament at Bristol in September 1293 to celebrate the wedding of his daughter, Eleanor, to Count Henri III of Bar. Nobles also laid on tournaments to entertain their wedding guests, as we have seen in the example of Duke Philip the Good of Burgundy in 1430.

The tournament was also considered fitting for a royal coronation. King Edward II of England had a tournament at his

▼ *The tournament survived into the 17th century. This one was held in Turin in 1619 to mark the marriage of Victor, Duke of Savoy and Prince of Piedmont, to Christine, third daughter of King Henry IV of France.*

coronation in Westminster in February 1308. Farther afield, at Acre in 1286, the crusaders fought an Arthurian 'Round Table' tournament in honour of the coronation of King Hugh III of Cyprus as King of Jerusalem. Events were also a frequent addition to diplomatic meetings as late as 1520 – King Francis I of France and King Henry VIII of England met with ceremony, feasting and jousting at the Field of the Cloth of Gold near Calais in France.

Tournaments were also associated with festivals of the Church year – particularly at Shrovetide, the celebrations prior to the self-denial of Lent, as well as at Easter and Christmas. Sometimes tournaments were also held in late autumn, prior to the onset of winter, notably on St Martin's Day, 11 November, the festival of the 4th-century churchman Martin of Tours.

Tournaments could last for a week or more, often beginning on Monday or Tuesday. They were not held on Sundays or Fridays, which were kept sacred, or on holy days of the Church calendar.

SEEKING GLORY

Between the 11th and 13th centuries knights would often travel in search of tournaments. Young noblemen and royals such as King Henry II of England's sons Henry the Young King and Geoffrey, Duke of Brittany, kept a permanent group of knights and squires for competing. In the summer of 1260, the 21-year-old Prince Edward (the future Edward I) travelled to France with a company of 80 companions to seek glory by fighting in tournaments – surprisingly, given his later status as a warrior, with little success. At this time it is probable that events were publicized by word of mouth among the participants, who before leaving at the end of a tourney would arrange to meet again in the future at a particular time and place.

More formal arrangements for planning and publicizing the events came into use in the 14th and 15th centuries. King René I of Naples, known as René d'Anjou and an artist and poet as well as a patron, gave details of tournament organization in his book *Le Livre des Tournois* (*The Book of Tournaments*), written in c.1450.

ISSUING A CHALLENGE

Often letters were sent out to particular knights to advise them of a coming tournament. Heralds rode out to proclaim the date, place and duration of the tournament; the rules under which it would be fought; the type of arms and armour to be used; and the arrangement of the tournament area – known as the lists. This would be announced at least a fortnight before the tournament was due to start.

Sometimes an invitation to a particular knight was issued by a challenge: the herald would ride to the court of the king, prince or noble knight to be invited, and present to him a blunt sword (the kind used in some tournaments), and taking the sword would signify acceptance of the challenge by the recipient. It was expected

▶ *In the close and highly dangerous combat of the mêlée, brute strength counted for as much as skill. This manuscript depicts a German tournament of the early 1300s.*

that he swear to fight not out of anger or a desire for violence, but in order to please his challengers and the ladies of the tournament court. The recipient then chose four judges of the tournament from a list of eight carried by the herald.

Invitations were often sent far and wide. For King Edward III of England's 1344 tournament at Windsor, the invitation was proclaimed by heralds as far afield as Brabant (in the Netherlands), Burgundy, Flanders, France, Hainault (in the Low Countries) and Scotland. Knights were promised safe conduct to and from the event. For a 1358 tournament, Edward spent £32 on sending heralds to Scotland, Flanders, Brabant, Germany and France.

GATHERING FOR THE EVENT

The knights who wanted to take part in a tournament gathered at least four days before the event was due to start. The

▼ *Knights usually made sure they could be identified in the lists by their coat of arms on shields and horse coverings. Occasionally knights deliberately avoided being identified – and competed as 'an unknown knight'.*

more important would make a formal processional entry into the city or town where the event was taking place. The appointed judges were required to take up residence in a local monastery or other religious establishment. All the knights planning to fight had to display their escutcheon, or shield, bearing their coat of arms, in the window of the inn and in the courtyard of the judges' residence. They also had to display it on the place they were staying, whether that was a room or a tent.

This gave knights or others the chance to make a complaint against particular contestants: a 'blot on the escutcheon' was a stain on a knight's reputation. On the eve of the contest the shields were inspected by the judges and if a complaint were upheld, then the knight in question would be excluded. There were a number of complaints liable to cause exclusion – for example being a proven murderer or a fugitive, having slandered a woman or broken a knight's duty to be honest, or having been excommunicated.

Tournaments also attracted merchants, who would gather in the days before jousting started. These included horse traders, sellers of fine clothes and moneylenders offering knights help in covering a possible ransom. Entertainers such as jugglers and fortune tellers also attended, giving the events the atmosphere of a fair.

THE LISTS

Lists, usually rectangular or oval, were set out within barriers either in a town – perhaps the marketplace – or in open countryside. Stands were set up for noble spectators. A strong wooden barrier was built around the lists to keep the spectators safe. This soon became a double fence, and in the area between the fences the squires stood, ready to rush to the assistance of the knights whom they served. The ground in lists was covered with dung, straw and sometimes sand.

A SEA OF COLOURS

THE PAGEANTRY OF THE TOURNAMENT

Tournaments were a magnificent sight, drenched in gorgeous colours, full of dramatic movement. They also had the extra spice of the passions of courtly love between knight and lady, and the promise of martial combat, even serious violence.

From specially constructed stands or balconies decorated with pennants and tapestries, lavishly dressed ladies and eager courtiers looked down on the knights and the poorer spectators gathered below, sometimes throwing coins into the crowd as an expression of their benevolence. Pavilions, also decked with flags, often lined the edge of the lists – the area laid out for competition. The knights wore elaborate armour sometimes decked only with the 'tokens' – the scarves, gloves or veils – of the ladies they represented, sometimes partly covered with colourful surcoats bearing the armorial bearings that adorned their shield as well as the horse-cloths and trappings. Heralds, who were familiar with the coats of arms of the contestants, proclaimed the names of knights as they entered the lists. We draw much of our knowledge of tournaments from accounts in chansons and romances, which presented an idealized version of tourneying. In practice, of course, there was great variety in the type of tournaments held, and many must have been far less splendid than the very grand ones glorified in chivalric literature.

FIGHTING IN COSTUME

Display was central to the event. Knights often fought in disguise, dressed as monks, cardinals, ancient Romans and women – but most often as knights from chivalric literature. When assuming a character, knights must have had a 'costume' simple enough to slip over their armour without affecting their ability to fight – perhaps a simple coat bearing a crest or arms, plus a symbol on horsecloths and trappings.

▼ *The colour and excitement of tournaments are evident in this scene from a 14th-century event. A herald (right) is master of ceremonies; in the grandstands, ladies and courtiers debate the outcome.*

Frequently, in the 13th–15th centuries, tournaments were devised as theatrical celebrations of chivalry, and those taking part either represented great knights of history or played out typical scenes from romance literature. In 1468 Charles the Bold, Duke of Burgundy, celebrated his third marriage, to Princess Margaret of York, with a lavish 14-day tournament at Bruges. It was set within a romance narrative, based on the story of Florimont, the Knight of the Golden Tree, whose service was to the Lady of the Secret Isle. A tree was erected in the market place in Bruges and a champion knight defended it against four challengers every day for eight days. The tree was guarded by a dwarf dressed in white and red satin and by a giant; each challenger had to knock four times on a barrier and identify himself to a herald before taking a lance from those proffered. He would then fight in the lists with the Knight of the Golden Tree, for a defined period of 30 minutes: the knight who broke the largest number of lances was to be the winner. The dwarf sounded a horn to begin the 30-minute challenge. After the eight days of jousting the tournament culminated in a mêlée for two competing teams of 25 knights on the final day.

Ladies and courtiers watching the main action of the tournament also dressed in costume and finery. To preside over her wedding jousts Princess Margaret, for instance, wore a glorious golden coronet set with pearls and precious stones and the white roses of York made from enamel – with her initials and those of Duke Charles picked out alongside lovers' knots.

ARTHURIAN 'ROUND TABLES'
There was a whole series of 'Round Table' tournaments in which knights played the parts of Arthur's leading warriors. In 1223 the crusader knight John of Ibelin, Lord of Beirut, held the first, a 'Round Table' in Cyprus to celebrate the knighting of his son. The German Ulrich von Lichtenstein took part in one at Neustadt in 1240, when six knights from his 'Round Table' fought against 17 attackers; it was planned

as jousting, one to one, but was fought rather more loosely, with knights competing two against one, in an event halfway between a joust and a mêlée. The fighting was fierce – Ulrich records that more than 100 spears ended up broken.

King Edward I of England held two 'Round Table' tournaments – once while a prince (in 1254) and once as king (in 1284). Perhaps the most celebrated of all is the one held at Windsor by Edward III of England in 1244, where he announced the formation of a secular chivalric brotherhood. The Most Noble Order of the Garter was formed four years later, in June 1348: it consisted of 26 knights, Edward and his son, the Black Prince, with 12 companions each.

SCENERY, PROPS AND DANCING
These events used props and scenery as well as costumes. It is probable, for instance, that the celebrated 5.5m (18ft)-diameter Round Table at Winchester was made for Edward III to use at one of his Arthurian tournaments; the design on the table, which features the names of Arthur's knights, was painted in the mid-16th century, probably for another royal devotee of chivalry, King Henry VIII. In 1328 Roger Mortimer, Earl of March, erected a castle

▲ *In the evenings, after vigorous exercise in the lists, the knights joined their ladies for courtly entertainments, dancing and feasting. The lower part of this fresco of c.1390 depicts this other part of tourneying.*

made from canvas as scenery for one of the tournaments he arranged to celebrate his engineering of the accession of the teenage Edward III to replace Edward II (the deposed king was later horribly murdered in Berkeley Castle, Gloucestershire). At the tournament held in 1430 by Philip the Good, described in the introduction to this chapter, there were many 'stage props' and large amounts of scenery, including a vast wooden lion and sculptures of a stag and a unicorn that dispensed drinks.

Such tournaments were important social events in the medieval calendar. They were accompanied by feasting and dancing from as early as the 12th century – we know that there was dancing at the tournaments in which William Marshal (1146–1219) competed. It became a tradition for there to be dancing on the night before the tournament began, and at many events – such as during a celebrated tournament held at Chauvency, France, in 1285 – there was dancing every night.

QUEEN OF THE TOURNAMENT
THE IMPORTANCE OF LADIES TO THE EVENT

Ladies played a central role in the tournament. As well as providing an audience, they were often patronesses of tournaments, which were proclaimed as being held in their honour, and served as inspiration for the competing knights. They were also, nominally at least, judges of the jousting and often awarded prizes to the best-performing knights.

A GLAMOROUS AUDIENCE
The first tournaments were more military manoeuvres than courtly entertainments and did not cater for audiences, but ladies were increasingly present as spectators and as patronesses of tournaments from the 13th century. The first record of an event held to honour a lady is from 1207, when Peter II of Aragon hosted a tournament at Montpellier to bring glory to his mistress.

In England the presence of ladies at tournaments was certainly the norm by

▼ *The king and queen look on from the royal box as two knights break their lances in combat. Note the sturdy wooden barrier (the 'tilt') built down the centre of the lists.*

c.1330. King Edward III's queen, Philippa of Hainault, was a regular attendee at her husband's tournaments after their marriage in 1328 and she probably helped popularize the attendance of noble ladies at the events. Earlier than this, however, English ladies were involved in themed events; for

▲ *Within the code of courtly love, a knight was driven to acts of bravery in tournament and in battle by the fact that his passion for his lady was pure and impossible.*

example, King Edward I of England's Round Table at Kenilworth Castle in 1279 was for 100 knights and their ladies.

As we have seen, tournaments were very often associated with grand courtly celebrations with dancing and feasting. King Edward III's great tournament at Windsor in 1344 began with a feast in the castle for the queen and her ladies, while the knights ate equally lavishly in specially erected pavilions. After the banquet came an evening of dancing; the jousting took place over the following three days.

ARTHUR'S QUEEN
In the elaborate tournaments planned on Arthurian and other themes, ladies took a part as queen, princess or damsel within the chivalric make-believe. At Le Hem, Picardy, in 1278 a two-day Arthurian tournament was held in honour of a lady portraying Queen Guinevere; it was

described in some detail in the poem 'Le Roman du Hem' written by an Anglo-Norman *trouvère* named Sarrasin. All the knights had to bring a lady with them, as a knight-errant in a romance would bring a damsel, and the tournament was opened by Dame Courtoisie ('Lady Courtesy').

The tournament, held by the lords of Bazentin and Longueval, provided a narrative setting for the jousting. At the start, seven knights of Guinevere humbled themselves before their queen, reporting that they had all been bested by a noble warrior named the Knight with the Lion. Immediately, this knight arrived, bringing a number of damsels in Guinevere's service, whom he had saved from a dreadful fate, and also a live lion. He was intended to represent Yvain, and was played by Robert II, Count of Artois, a devoted tourneyer who took part in the event despite having been excommunicated for attending tournaments while they were officially banned. He would later lead the French army to a heavy defeat by the Flemish at the Battle of Courtrai in 1302.

Subsequently, a noble lady claimed that these knights of Guinevere were the best in the world, but her lord angrily challenged her and ordered her to be beaten in public. Guinevere's knights were then able to prove themselves by defeating this lady's champion one at a time. The event was less a performance before an audience than a shared theatrical experience, for all those present were required to act in the pretence that these events were taking place at the court of King Arthur.

THE LADY AS INSPIRATION

As the courtly love tradition developed, knights often fought to honour a lady. The knight would enter the lists wearing a 'favour' – a token such as a scarf that she had given him. The knight's desire to win the lady's favour inspired him to fight more bravely. She became his protector. In Thomas Malory's *Morte d'Arthur*, Sir Palomides – who, like Sir Tristan, loves Iseult – becomes unbeatable in the lists after a glimpse of Iseult laughing in a window overlooking the contest – 'he struck down with his sword or his spear every knight he encountered'. In this case, Palomides is inspired, despite the fact that Iseult's love is for Tristan – the laugh he saw was prompted by the sight of Sir Tristan riding past in his knightly finery.

▲ *A knight pays homage to the lady who is presiding over the tournament. These brief, formal encounters, bound by convention, were the very stuff of chivalric romance.*

PRIZEGIVERS

The lady or ladies presiding over an event were often asked to give prizes for the best performances in the mêlée and the jousts. Some accounts suggest that they chose the winners, but it is more likely that they just presented the prizes to winners who were chosen by heralds and other nominated judges familiar with the complex rules and scoring for a tournament.

▼ *This illustration of a 15th-century Italian tournament depicts the knights competing fiercely in a mêlée.*

WAR AND PEACE

TOURNEYS ON CAMPAIGN AND PEACETIME REGULATION OF EVENTS

Jousts and mêlées were often fought by knights during wartime as a diversion while they were far from their home on a campaign. In peacetime, because of the not infrequent deaths and attendant violence, tournaments provoked opposition from state and Church authorities.

JOUSTS OF WAR

From the very earliest days of tournaments, knights fought mêlées and jousts during military campaigns – particularly at a time of truce or during the longueurs of a siege. We have seen that, according to chronicler Geoffrey of Malaterra, Norman knights fought a tournament during a siege in Sicily as early as 1062; in the 12th century, jousts were held during sieges at Würzburg (Germany) in 1127, and at Lincoln during the siege of the castle by King Stephen's forces in January–February 1141; and in 1197, the army of Richard I held a tournament at Tours during a truce. Other examples include that of the great Breton knight Bertrand du Guesclin, who

▼ *Although the Church disapproved of them, tournaments were often a recruiting ground for holy war, when knights agreed to undertake a crusade to the Holy Land.*

in 1357 at Rennes fought a series of jousts against an English opponent, while he was also masterminding the defence of the town against a besieging English army commanded by Henry of Grosmont, Duke of Lancaster.

In England's 14th-century border conflicts with Scotland there were often prolonged periods of inactivity between engagements because the Scots used guerrilla tactics and could be difficult to engage. Knights from opposite sides arranged to hold jousts of war during these periods, which were neither really truces nor periods of full war. In 1341 at Berwick, jousts between 20 knights on each side left three dead and many injured, but nevertheless were ended with the giving of prizes to the best knights, as if it were a peacetime tournament.

CHIVALRIC ARENA OR DEN OF SINNERS?

For a knight the tournament was the chivalric arena par excellence in peacetime, a place in which he could display the key chivalric virtues of *prouesse* (prowess) and courage in fighting, and *courtoisie* (courtesy) in his dealings with the ladies; he could show *franchise* and *debonnaireté*

▲ *Pope Innocent II, who banned tourneying in 1130, had to use violence in his struggle to win the papacy from rival claimant Anacletus II. Innocent sent German king Lothair II to Italy to fight on his behalf.*

(good breeding and noble manners), and exhibit *largesse* (generosity) in dealing generously with crowds at the tournament.

For the Church, on the other hand, the tournament was a sinful indulgence in violence and pride. In the mid-13th century the bishop of Acre wrote that knights at a tournament committed all of the seven deadly sins, for they felt pride when they were praised, and envy when others were lauded more highly; they allowed themselves to feel and act on anger in the combat of the lists; they were avaricious because they greedily eyed the horses and shining equipment of other knights; they indulged in lust when they set out to please ungodly women by wearing their favours; they were slothful when they were defeated and slunk back to their quarters; and they were gluttonous at the feasting that followed the fighting.

In the light of this sermonizing, it would appear that at a 1362 tournament in Cheapside, London, seven knights meant mischief when they entered the lists in the guise of the seven deadly sins and fought against challengers.

TOURNAMENTS BANNED

Pope Innocent II banned tournaments in 1130. At the Council of Clermont in that year he declared: 'we firmly prohibit those detestable markets or fairs at which knights … show off their strength and boldness,' adding that aside from the real danger of death or serious injury there were many 'dangers to the soul' in attending a tournament. Those who ignored the prohibition risked excommunication. Knights killed at tournaments were denied a church burial.

Kings added their authority to that of the Church in outlawing tourneying. The bans were of variable effectiveness: in England, strong kings such as Henry I and Henry II were able to enforce their will but a weak ruler such as King Stephen could not, and as a result in the reigns of the two Henrys (1100–35 and 1154–89), English knights routinely travelled to France to tourney, while under King Stephen (1135–54), knights took on themselves the right to fight at tournaments and Stephen could do nothing about it.

REGULATION OF TOURNAMENTS

In 1194 King Richard I of England defied the papal ban and introduced a licensing arrangement under which tournaments could be legally held in England. Richard, though a great knight and a devoted chivalric patron, was not himself a keen tourneyer. While in France, before he was king, he devoted his martial energies to fighting wars in the duchy of Aquitaine rather than competing in tournaments. But he reputedly saw the benefit of tournaments as training for knights, and wanted to establish them in England to improve military skills.

Under Richard's scheme there were to be five licensed tournament areas in England: Wiltshire, Warwickshire, Suffolk, Northamptonshire and Nottinghamshire. A knight who wished to hold a tournament in one of these areas had to buy a charter and a personal licence. Knights from outside England were not permitted. Historians note that Richard I was continually short of funds as king, due partly to his expensive crusading campaigns, and no doubt designed the scheme partly because of the income it would generate through licences and charters – and also through the hefty fines imposed on those who ignored the regulations.

▲ Depictions of dancing (bottom) and feasting (top) join riding out to war and competing in tournaments among the works of the devil in this illustration from an early 14th-century manuscript.

In France, where the kings had a closer relationship with the papacy, kings continued to ban tourneying – with little effect. The papal ban on the sport stayed in place until it was eventually lifted in 1316 by Pope John XXII, the second pope of the Avignon Papacy (the period in the 14th century when seven successive popes, all French, made their residence at Avignon in France).

DEATH AND DANGER

THE RISK OF DEFEAT IN A TOURNAMENT

Especially in the early years, tournaments were dangerous and knights were sometimes killed in the full-blooded encounters of the mêlée. Even in later, more stylized events, a knight's defeat in a tournament could bring ruin and humiliation, severe injury or occasionally death.

KILLED IN THE LISTS

Several knights died as a result of the conditions in which early tournaments were fought. Some were killed by frightened or stampeding horses – King Henry II of England's fourth son, Geoffrey, Duke of Brittany, was trampled to death in 1186 at a tournament near Paris. Sometimes, in hot and dry conditions, the heat and dust during a tournament could be overpowering – in 1241 at Neuss, in Germany, as many as 80 knights died from suffocation.

Many knights also lost their lives because of the force of the conflict. In 1344 Sir William Montagu, 1st Earl of

▼ *The shuddering impact between two knights hurls one to the ground. This graphic woodcut of c.1516 is thought to be by the great German artist Albrecht Dürer.*

Salisbury, died from severe bruising he had received after fighting in a tournament at Windsor. The Montagu family suffered badly in this regard – in 1383 Sir William's grandson, another Sir William Montagu, also died from wounds received in a Windsor tournament – the injuries were delivered by his own father Sir William Montagu, the 2nd Earl, a veteran of the Battle of Poitiers and one of the first Knights of the Garter. Earlier, in 1252, Sir Roger of Leybourne killed Sir Arnulf de

▲ *The main danger in the lists was being injured in the head by the other knight's lance. Jousters might also be badly hurt if knocked at high speed from the saddle.*

Munteny, a knight in King Henry III of England's household, in a tournament at Walden. Sir Roger, seeking revenge for a slight by Sir Arnulf at an earlier tournament, used a sharpened lance, which struck Sir Arnulf under the helmet. Sir Roger recovered from this early disgrace by taking the cross and going on crusade. He succeeded in winning the king's forgiveness, and had a long and chequered chivalric career, fighting both with Simon de Montfort and for the royalist cause in the 1260s.

TRAGIC ACCIDENT

Late in the history of chivalry, King Henry II of France sustained a fatal injury while jousting in July 1559. The tournament, in the Place des Vosges in Paris, was held to celebrate his daughter's marriage to King Philip II of Spain, as well as the Peace Treaty of Cateau-Cambrésis that ended the Italian War of 1551–59. During a joust the lance carried by Henry's opponent, Gabriel, Count of Montgomery, shattered – and a piece of it went through the king's

▲ *With pride, a great deal of status and personal safety at stake, jousts and subsequent sword fights could become very heated. Judges were on hand to intervene if a contest got out of hand.*

visor and through his brain. The king lived for nine days in agony, and although he was able to absolve Gabriel of blame, the royal physicians were unable to save him and he succumbed to the injury.

JOUSTS OF WAR

Several died in the jousts of war that were fought between knights during breaks in military campaigns. In 1341 Scottish knight Sir William Douglas was killed in a joust between four Scottish and four English knights at Roxburgh. In 1351 in the celebrated Combat of the Thirty, two teams of 30 knights competed near Ploërmel, Brittany: a French force of 30 Bretons against an English group of English, Germans and Bretons. (The two groups were garrisons attached to rival lords disputing possession of the duchy of Brittany.) In this event, at least three of the French knights were killed, while no fewer than nine of the English knights died including the English commander, Sir Robert Bramborough.

RUIN IN DEFEAT

When a knight was unhorsed, his opponent had to dismount to continue the fight: the pair abandoned their lances and fought on with maces and swords. They would fight until one was unable to carry on through injury or exhaustion and cried 'quits' to end the contest. A judge or patron(ess) of a fight could also intervene to stop it. A defeated knight was liable to pay a ransom for his freedom and would also be expected to give up his horse, his armour and his weapons. To be released he had to pledge to raise the ransom fee – he would give his *parole* (word of honour) to do this, and be released 'on parole'.

A knight who was repeatedly defeated would soon build up a sizeable debt in promised ransoms. The 15th-century French nobleman Robert de Baudricourt reported of a relative who often lost at tournaments and was able to survive only because his wife, remaining behind on the family estate, was so careful with the money that she was able to meet these commitments on his behalf. On the other hand, a knight who regularly won could quickly build a fortune – not through the acquisition of prizes, which were small, but through ransoms and seizing his opponent's arms, armour and horses.

JOUSTS *À OUTRANCE*, JOUSTS *À PLAISANCE*

The jousts of war were the most dangerous form of the sport, fought with sharpened weapons, and clearly in some encounters to the death. They were termed jousts *à outrance* ('to the uttermost'). Alongside them in the 14th and 15th centuries courtly tournaments were often fought *à plaisance* ('for the pleasure of the encounter'), with blunted ('rebated') lances, maces and swords.

▼ *At tournaments, even with blunted weapons, deaths were common.*

'THE GREATEST KNIGHT THAT EVER LIVED'

SIR WILLIAM MARSHAL

Sir William Marshal rose from humble origins to become a great knight and statesman, initially establishing his reputation through his astonishing prowess at tournaments. Some claim that in the many tournaments he fought he remained undefeated. Stephen Langton, Archbishop of Canterbury (1207–28), declared him 'the greatest knight that ever lived'.

After Sir William's death in 1219, his son William Marshal II and his squire and executor John d'Earley commissioned a biography of the great man. The result, *L'Histoire du Guillaume le Maréchal*, was a 19,214-line poem, written in rhyming couplets, giving a full account of the exploits of this remarkable figure.

AN EARLY ESCAPE

In 1152, aged just six, William was given up as hostage by his father John Marshal when John's castle at Newbury was besieged by the army of King Stephen. The king lifted the blockade, expecting surrender negotiations to begin, but John – apparently untroubled about the safety of his son – instead used the opportunity to bring provisions into the castle. Stephen

◄ *King Stephen, who threatened to kill the 6-year-old William in order to force the co-operation of his father, John Marshal.*

tried several times to convince John that he would kill young William if he did not co-operate but John reputedly replied: 'I have a hammer and anvil on which I can forge better sons than he!' In the end, Stephen spared William and kept him at court as a royal ward until 1153.

In *c.*1159–66 William underwent his chivalric education as a squire at the court of William de Tancarville, Chamberlain of Normandy, who was his mother's cousin. In 1166, aged about 20, he was knighted. His first engagement was in war, that same year, when with de Tancarville and as part of the garrison of the castle at Neufchâtel-en-Bray, he fought in a frontier war between King Henry II and the counts of Boulogne, Flanders and Ponthieu. His bravery almost got the better of him – his master called him back at one stage of the conflict and told him not to be a 'hothead', and he lost his horse to an opponent.

HIS FIRST TOURNAMENT

He was at a low ebb. De Tancarville, clearly displeased, refused to supply him with a new horse and he was of such

▲ *William Marshal was largely responsible for raising the first stone fortifications at Pembroke Castle in Wales. He built on the site of a wooden structure erected in 1093.*

limited means himself that he had to sell his clothes to procure one. But shortly afterwards, his life changed when he fought in his first tournament, at Le Mans. He was an immediate success: in the mêlée he captured a number of prisoners including a notable Scottish courtier, and at the end was richer to the tune of four horses, with a half-share in another.

William spent two years, 1167–68, winning repeatedly (and growing rich) on the tournament circuit of France. He went into partnership with another talented knight in the party of King Henry II's second son, Henry the Young King. In ten months, William and his partner captured no fewer than 103 knights along with their horses and equipment.

In 1168 William entered the service of his uncle, Patrick, Earl of Salisbury, and while fighting on his side in Poitou was injured and captured by soldiers serving Guy de Lusignan (the French knight who later became king of Jerusalem). William was imprisoned, but was ransomed by Henry II's queen, Eleanor of Aquitaine.

ROYAL SERVICE AND CRUSADES

In 1170 William was appointed tutor in arms to the 15-year-old Henry the Young King. Over the next decade they fought together often at tournaments and William became rich enough to maintain his own household knights. However, he was banished from the Young King's court in 1182, accused of having become too intimate with the Young King's wife, Margaret. This was probably a false accusation put about by jealous courtiers, but we cannot be sure.

The following year Henry and Marshal were reconciled and Marshal returned but only in time to see the Young King die of dysentery in June 1183. The Young King had taken the cross, and on his deathbed he gave William Marshal his cloak and made him promise to take it to Jerusalem. William thereafter went on crusade, and in the Holy Land made a solemn vow that his burial would be as a Knight Templar.

FIGHTING THE COEUR DE LION

On his return to Europe he served King Henry II from 1186 until the king's death in July 1189. Marshal fought in the king's household guard on campaigns against Philip II of France and Henry's rebellious

▼ *Temple Church, London, where William Marshal was buried in 1219.*

sons. He reputedly had the chance to kill Prince Richard (the future King Richard I of England) when the latter was suddenly isolated – an encounter between perhaps the two most celebrated chivalric men of the 12th century. Richard is said to have begged for his life and Marshal chose to kill the rebel prince's horse instead.

As king, Richard chose to honour Marshal. In 1189 he arranged Marshal's marriage to the 17-year-old Isabel de Clare, heiress to Richard de Clare, 2nd Earl of Pembroke. Marshal, now a great magnate, undertook substantial building at the de Clares' Pembroke and Chepstow castles.

PROMINENT NOBLE

For the rest of his long life, Marshal was one of the leading men in England. He was on the council of regency while King Richard I was away on the Third Crusade (1189–92), then was named Marshal of the Kingdom. After Richard's death he served King John, supported Magna Carta (he was a signatory) and on John's death was named as Protector of the Kingdom during the minority of King Henry III.

He was by now an old man of 70, but still fought with astonishing vigour in Henry's army against the rebel barons at the Battle of Lincoln of 1217. He died in 1219 and, in fulfilment of his vow while he was on crusade, was invested as a Knight Templar on his deathbed. He is buried in the Temple Church in London, where a fine effigy of this great knight lies with those of his sons.

▲ *The signing of Magna Carta by King John in June 1215. Sir William Marshal was also a signatory.*

WILLIAM MARSHAL
Born: *c.*1146
Died: 14 May 1219
Knighted: 1166
Famous for: sparing Richard Coeur de Lion's life and rising from obscurity to be Marshal of the Kingdom
Greatest achievement: remained undefeated in European tournaments

▼ *The effigy of William Marshal in Temple Church, London.*

RULES OF THE GAME
TOURNAMENT LAWS AND TECHNIQUES

The rules governing the fighting in a tournament were created as the sport developed. If the first tournaments were effectively war without the killing, the more refined events that took place from the mid-15th century onwards were governed by complex rules. These covered how to score points, and detailed the manoeuvres that were illegal and would lead to disqualification.

WAR GAMES

In tournaments of the 12th century, as in the Franks' very first countryside battles of the mid-11th century, knights could use any techniques to unhorse and then defeat an opponent, but should not fight to the death nor deliberately aim even to injure one another. There were fenced-off areas where engagement was suspended and knights could take a rest for their horses or themselves. In these early tournaments ordinary weapons were used – knights

▼ *By the 15th century tournaments were much better regulated, with rules of entry, engagement and scoring.*

could use lances, swords, battle-axes, maces, and bows and arrows.

Some of the techniques and tactics reported seem scarcely chivalrous. For example, the 12th-century noble Philip of Alsace, Count of Flanders, was renowned for refusing to take part in the mêlée until the other knights involved were near to exhaustion – he would then sweep into the lists to attack a group of opponents from the flank and claim a large number of easy ransoms. (Philip later went twice on crusade, once in 1177, and once in 1190 on the Third Crusade, when he died during the Siege of Acre from sickness.)

RULES OF ENGAGEMENT

There exists only limited evidence of the rules of engagement for tournaments in the 13th and 14th centuries. It would seem that there was a developing set of general rules and also that rules were agreed for individual tournaments. At the 'Round Table' events, so popular in the 13th century and afterwards, knights agreed to rules laid down when they entered the tournament.

Typical rules in these 'Round Table' tournaments specified the use of blunted weapons, and said that knights should not have concealed weapons. They also set the limit on the number of squires who were allowed to enter the lists to assist a knight in the tournament, and usually required that the squires and all other supporting retainers must be unarmed. The rules often declared that once a knight had surrendered he could not be attacked further, or launch another attack himself. The early 13th century saw the first use of blunted weapons, which greatly helped in making the combat in tournaments safer, and the rounded coronal head was used on the lance in place of a point from the mid-13th century.

The rules usually also laid down details about the kind of armour worn and the length of the lance. It was the normal practice for knights to use lances supplied by the defending knight to ensure that they were both fighting with identical equipment and challengers could gain no secret advantage by using their own weapon. It is known from the account in the romance of Fulk Fitzwarin (*c*.1230) that judges were in charge of settling any disputes in the tournament by the early to mid-13th century.

SCORES AND DISQUALIFICATION

Complex scoring rules were in use at some tournaments by the mid-15th century. They are detailed in Sir John Tiptoft's *Ordinances* of 1466. According to this list, the best score was achieved by the knight who knocked his opponent from his horse and brought the horse down with him. The next best point-scoring move was to make two spears break by the collision of their coronals or rounded tips. The third best score was achieved by hitting an opponent's visor three times, and the fourth best score was gained by breaking the largest number of spears.

TECHNIQUES IN THE LISTS

Duarte, King of Portugal, wrote a manual on jousting and the management of horses, *The Art of Good Horsemanship*, in 1434. The book contains detailed advice on how to hold and support the lance, the best type of equipment to use, the training methods needed for effective jousting and even, perhaps most interestingly, on the mental strength needed to supplement physical bravery if a knight were to succeed in jousting.

Duarte stresses the importance of balancing the lance and, among a number of options for carrying it, suggests that the best way in a tournament is on the leg, supported by a bag placed on the saddle bow or on the leg itself. He adds that a knight should never use a lance that is too heavy for him to handle comfortably. He writes that it is a useful technique to aim slightly below the point of impact – this method enables a knight to see the exact place he intends to strike as clearly as possible, and prevents the frequent error of pulling the lance too far down at the last moment.

In addition, King Duarte stresses that it is important to banish fear and to maintain steadfast commitment in the lists: many jousters fail, he writes, because they look away or close their eyes or pull the lance imperceptibly off target just prior to impact. But it is important, he adds, not to be too tense because this may also cause the jouster to pull the lance off target. A knight should be confident in his abilities and able to ride into the impact with his eyes open and trained right to the last on the place on his opponent he intends to hit. Furthermore, he adds, a knight should never seek unfair advantage – and if he perceives that he is far better equipped than his opponent, he should lower his shield to even things up a little. He writes: 'I believe that you cannot prove yourself a skilled jouster if you are unwilling to take a risk.'

▲ *Charles the Bold, Duke of Burgundy (1433–77), dressed in the splendid robes of the Order of the Golden Fleece.*

We have seen that in the 1468 tournament in Bruges held by Charles the Bold, Duke of Burgundy, the knights jousted for a set period of 30 minutes, measured on an hourglass, and the winner was the one who broke the most lances. However, this arrangement was unusual, and completely unknown in tournaments before the mid-15th century, when knights generally competed for a set number of jousts, agreed in advance.

Sir John Tiptoft's *Ordinances* also indicated that a knight could be disqualified if he struck a horse, struck an unarmed knight or one who had turned his back, hit the tilt (the central barrier in the competition area) three times, or took off his helmet twice, unless this was caused by trouble with his mount. When fighting in a general mêlée, knights were required to give up their sword for inspection by the judges before entering the fight, and they could be disqualified if they dropped a sword, tied the sword to their hand, hit an opponent beneath the waist with a pike, or rested on the barrier.

▼ *The squire's role in a tournament was an important one, and tourney rules reflected this by including various regulations on how many squires could attend, and how they should be armed.*

PROTECTION IN THE LISTS

TOURNAMENT ARMOUR AND EQUIPMENT

In the tournaments of the 11th and 12th centuries and for much of the 13th century, knights used the same armour and equipment in tournaments as they did in battle. Conditions of combat in a mêlée were similar to those on a battlefield, so there was no need to develop specialist tournament equipment. But from the late 13th century, the elite armour makers who

▼ *In early tournaments knights wore chain mail, often with a surcoat for identification over the top. The great helm gave better protection but restricted the wearer's view.*

served kings, princes and leading knights began to make specialist armour and other equipment designed for use in jousting.

EARLY ARMOUR

Knights at the first tournaments wore a chain mail hauberk and camail, or mail hood, with a simple conical helmet with nose piece of the kind shown on Norman knights in the Bayeux Tapestry. Gradually they began to use chain mail sleeves that also protected the wrist and hand – although the palms were necessarily left exposed to make it easier to hold and manipulate the lance and other weapons.

A full helmet design was introduced in the late 12th or early 13th century, and is commonly known as the 'great helmet'. These helmets were generally flat-topped and cylindrical in shape and provided much better protection, but had definite drawbacks – it was very hard to see out through the two small eye-slits, and also difficult to breathe through the holes situated near the mouth.

CRESTS AND COATS OF ARMS

When knights began wearing a full helmet, it became impossible to tell them apart. They started to sport armorial bearings to proclaim their identity. It was important to do so because the display of individual *prouesse* (prowess) was a key motive for fighting in the tournament. One of these identifiers was the crest, worn on top of the helmet. This could be a few feathers or else a heraldic beast or symbolic feature, made probably from cloth and wood. Another was the surcoat, a cloth garment worn over the armour and decorated with coats of arms.

LINEN AND LEATHER ARMOUR

A knight or soldier who received a heavy blow when wearing chain mail could be very badly bruised. In the 13th century, knights at tournament began to

▲ *A knight takes leave of his lady. He does not wear a surcoat but has his coat of arms emblazoned on his horsecloth.*

wear padded linen armour instead: as the use of blunted or rebated weapons spread, knights at tournament needed protection not against cutting and penetration, as they did in battle, but against bruising following heavy impact. Bruising was a very serious problem: Sir William Longespee was very badly bruised while jousting in 1256 and reportedly never fully recovered. Prince Edward (the future King Edward I of England) wore padded linen armour in his first tournament, at Blyth in 1258.

In the late 13th century, armour makers experimented with other materials including plates of metal, horn, whalebone and leather. The last of these became a popular choice – the leather was boiled and soaked in hot wax so it was soft enough to be fashioned into pieces that fitted tightly, but it was also sufficiently hard to repel a blow by a lance or sword, and it was light. Armour made from *cuir bouilli* (boiled leather) was popular until the 15th century; King Edward I of England held a bohort tournament at Windsor in 1258 in which participants were only permitted leather armour. A particularly popular piece of leather armour was the cuirass, a moulded piece that protected the chest, stomach and back, and was worn beneath the surcoat.

PLATE ARMOUR

As we have seen in Chapter Four, the first suits of plate armour, which appeared in *c*.1330, consisted of several plates of tempered steel, either laced in place or sewn on to a coat of leather or cloth and worn

▼ *Tournaments were flamboyant public displays of a knight's wealth, as well as their military prowess and skill, and helmet plumes became an expression of both.*

▶ *The two most common kinds of horse used for jousting were chargers and destriers. Chargers were medium-weight horses bred and trained for agility and stamina, while destriers were heavy war horses.*

beneath the surcoat. They also included gauntlets, sabatons or shoes, and pieces to protect the throat and the upper and lower arms. The first solid breastplates were developed very quickly, probably as early as *c*.1340.

SPECIALIST TOURNAMENT ARMOUR

At around the same time, amid this rapid development of new types of armour, there appeared the first pieces designed for use in tournaments. These included the *maindefer* and *poitrine pur justes* – we do not know for sure what they were, but they were probably a gauntlet made to hold a lance, and a breastplate with a support on which to rest the lance.

In the years of the late 14th

to the mid-15th century, knights could wear full suits of jointed plate armour. At this time, the original great helmet was widely replaced by a smaller design called the 'frog-mouthed helmet' (so called because of its profile), with a rounded top and curved front. As pageantry played an increasingly important role in tournaments, knights needed armour not only for protection but also to give them a splendid and glamorous appearance. Heraldic devices were emblazoned on surcoats and horse trappings, and elaborate, attention-seeking plumes adorned helms.

WEAPONS AND SHIELDS

In early mêlées and later jousts of war, knights fought with the ordinary weapons of contemporary warfare: lances, axes, maces and swords. In jousts of peace they used weapons with blunted blades; in

particular, the sharp end of the lance was replaced with a coronal, shaped like a tiny crown with three short protrusions, from the mid-13th century. In battle, knights of this era carried a triangular shield, but in jousts of peace they used the oval ecranché shield, which had a part missing on the right-hand side to allow aiming of the lance.

In the 16th and 17th centuries, as tournaments became displays more than contests, knights began to use mechanical devices that produced memorable effects for spectators. Chief among these was the spring-mounted shield that shattered dramatically into pieces when it was struck by the opponent's lance. During this period elite competitors such as King Henry VIII of England and the Holy Roman Emperor Maximilian I wore magnificent, highly ornamented jousting armour, with delicate chasing and fluting. This type of armour is so closely associated with the emperor that it is called 'Maximilian armour'.

BROTHERS IN ARMS
CHIVALRIC ORDERS AND TOURNAMENTS

Beginning in the mid-14th century, a number of lay chivalric brotherhoods were formed. They were modelled on the religious brotherhoods such as those of the Knights Templar and Knights Hospitallers, which had come into existence in the era of the First Crusade (1196–99). However, these lay orders required members to swear an oath of loyalty to their secular lord and to fight on his behalf in war. Most of these orders were closely connected to tournaments.

▼ *The cult of St George, a soldier in the Roman army who was martyred in AD303, was popularized by knights returning from the First Crusade. The story of George and the dragon was recast within the conventions of medieval chivalry, with the saint riding a white horse and using a lance.*

THE ORDER OF ST GEORGE
The first of these was probably the Order of St George, founded in Hungary by King Charles in 1325. It was a brotherly union of knights who swore to defend the realm and protect the king, and to follow him in 'pastimes and knightly sports' – doubtless a reference to tournaments they contested. Unlike the later orders, described below, the Order of St George did not have the monarch at its head.

THE ORDER OF THE BANDA
In 1332 in Vittoria, Castile, King Alfonso XI of Castile and León (r. 1312–50) established the first lay brotherhood of knights, the Order of the Banda – or Sash. The members wore a white surcoat with a broad vermilion sash running diagonally from the left shoulder down to the waist.

▲ *Knights at a session of the Order of the Golden Fleece, formed in 1430 by Philip the Good, Duke of Burgundy. Philip based the brotherhood on the Order of the Garter.*

They swore an oath of loyalty to the king, and were to be grouped together in an elite unit within the royal army when at war. They also promised to love their fellow knights as brothers, and to avoid conflict among themselves.

The order was specifically linked to fighting in tournaments: it was a duty for each member knight to attend any tournament within a day's ride of where he was if he were summoned by the king. Moreover, it was laid down as an expectation that every meeting of the order would include a tournament. Chronicle reports reveal that Alfonso was a dedicated tourneyer and believed tournaments to be a valuable means of keeping his knights trained up and ready for war. He made new members by giving a surcoat and sash to any knight who performed great deeds in war against his enemies.

At a tournament held in Valladolid at Easter 1334, Alfonso fought incognito among the Banda knights against a team of challengers. Great deeds of chivalry were performed, and the fighting became so heated that the four appointed judges had to break the contest up for fear that the king would be badly hurt – according to the chronicles, he was receiving bruising blows in the midst of the press. The combat then moved to a second location, at a bridge just outside the town, and again the judges had to break the fighting up because it was so fierce.

The knights of the Banda are also reported to have fought at the pilgrim destination of Santiago de Compostela in 1332 and many years later at a Christmas tournament in Seville held by King Henry II of Castile and León (r. 1369–79) in 1375. But the prime of the order lasted no more than 20 years, and after Alfonso's death in 1350 it was in decline although it continued to exist for around 100 years.

THE ORDER OF ST CATHERINE

Formed in the Dauphiné, south-eastern France, in the 1330s, the Order of St Catherine was another lay brotherhood. Its knights swore to serve the lord of the Dauphiné and were committed to help one another and to be ready to lend one another horses and jousting equipment at tournaments. They carried a shield bearing an image of St Catherine, and were required to attend celebrations on her feast day at Côte-St-André each year – only those who were not able-bodied or who were more than three days' journey distant were excused.

THE ORDER OF THE GARTER

The most celebrated of these lay orders is certainly the Most Noble Order of the Garter, established at Windsor Castle on St George's Day, 23 April, 1348 by King Edward III of England. It consisted of 26 knights – Edward and his son, the Black Prince, with 12 companions each.

Four years earlier, during a tournament held at Windsor, Edward had vowed to form an order of Arthurian knights called the Order of the Round Table. Initially, the plan was for 300 knights to be in the

▲ *These illustrations of the badges of King Edward III, Richard II and Henry IV are from Writhe's* Garter Book, *a late-15th-century heraldic and genealogical volume.*

order, but Edward had scaled down the plans (perhaps influenced by the Order of the Banda) by the time he created the Order of the Garter. The 1348 foundation established a college of 12 canons and an almshouse for impoverished knights at Windsor. The vows of the order required knights never to fight on opposing sides, never to leave England without the king's permission, and not to be seen in public without the insignia of the order – a dark blue garter. Edward inaugurated the order with a feast and tournament at Windsor. The founding knights were regular contestants at Edward's tournaments in this period – and most had fought alongside Edward and the Black Prince at the Battle of Crécy in 1346.

THE ORDER OF THE STAR

This French order was formed in 1352, with 500 knights. It was dedicated to the Virgin Mary, and its motto was *Monstrat regibus astra viam* ('Kings see their way by the stars'). Its stated aims were to promote chivalry and increase honour.

TOURNAMENT SOCIETIES

In Germany in the mid-14th century groups of knights would gather in tournament societies. Tournaments were organized among these groups, with one society issuing a challenge to another. A similar body was formed in England in 1344 by Henry, 3rd Earl of Lancaster. The knights in Henry's society made a commitment to meet for jousting at Lincoln once a year on Whit Monday, and under a royal licence they were permitted to hold tournaments even during times of war or during a general ban.

▼ *Early shields bore very simple designs.*

KNIGHTS OF GOOD STANDING

THE USES OF HERALDRY

From open beginnings in the 11th–12th centuries, tournaments became socially more exclusive. Heraldry, or the practice of making and displaying family coats of arms, developed alongside this evolution of the tournament.

KNIGHTLY HERITAGE

The earliest tournaments seem to have been open to all-comers, as long as they possessed a suit of chain mail armour. In practical terms, this often limited entry to knights and squires, and the rule that only knights could take part in tournaments was gradually formalized. This became the general rule in England, France and Spain, but did not hold everywhere – ordinary citizens would joust in the Baltic towns, in the Low Countries and in the cities of south Germany.

By the 14th century in England, France and Spain, tournaments were often only open to knights who could trace knightly ancestry back to their grandparents. In Germany, perhaps as a reaction to the involvement of citizens in some urban

▼ *The Heralds' Roll of shields and coats of arms was drawn up in England c.1270–80.*

jousts, even more highly exclusive tournaments began to be held, until by c.1480 only those whose forebears had actually been fighting in tournaments for three generations back (as far back as the great-grandfather) were permitted to take part in the tournaments. This was a reflection of a social change in the 14th and 15th centuries in which status resided ever increasingly in one's descent.

SOCIAL SHAMING

As we have seen, procedures were also introduced to exclude knights who were guilty of wrongdoing – such as adulterers, perjurers or robber knights. Exclusions also included those considered unworthy for social reasons – for example those who had married outside the nobility, illegitimate sons, traders and moneylenders.

In some tournaments the punishment for a knight found guilty of these offences was to beat him, confiscate his horse, then put him on his saddle on the barrier around the lists and make him stay there for the entire tournament. The same punishment lay in store for a knight who made accusations against another that proved to be false. In some of the most

▲ *These shields are from the Carlisle Roll, a heraldic document listing the 277 knights who took part in King Edward III's military campaign against Scotland in 1335.*

exclusive German tournaments, a knight could be beaten and excluded simply for not having the proof that his forebears had tourneyed within the past 50 years.

HERALDRY AND PROOF OF DESCENT

Heraldry developed from the need to identify oneself in battle or in the lists. The 'coat of arms' was so called because it was originally a surcoat or tunic emblazoned with a device and worn over the armour. The first coats of arms in the 13th century were simple stripes or crosses. Later ones usually included images of animals – typically lions, birds, boars, deer and dragons; flowers such as the fleur-de-lis and the rose were also popular. In time, knights also included representations of weapons or chivalric equipment such as swords, spurs and horseshoes. In tournaments knights generally bore their coats of arms on their shield, as well as on their surcoat and their horsecloths.

The first coats of arms were personal, but with the emphasis on descent they came to be treated as hereditary. As this process continued over generations, and families intermarried, coats of arms were combined. The combination of elements from two coats of arms was called compounding. This might be necessary if a knight married, acquired new property or received a particular honour. Quartering involved splitting a shield into four parts to combine the insignia of different coats of arms in one design.

THE ROLE OF HERALDS

Heralds began as public speakers, sent out to announce dates and times of tournaments, and were then required to act as commentators for the events themselves – to announce the arrival of particular knights in the lists and to interpret events for those watching. To do this job they had to be familiar with contestants' armorial bearings. As coats of arms became more complicated and more significant as a badge of knightly descent to allow entry into a tournament, heralds became acknowledged experts on family history and the technicalities of coats of arms. The heralds had to be well educated, knowledgeable about the arms of historical knights that had been established by convention, and the symbolism of colours, plants and animals used in the designs.

Initially heralds were probably itinerants who sought work at tournaments

▲ *In this scene of a tournament in the 14th century this herald is shown dressed in all his heraldic finery.*

when they were held, but they were soon attached to particular lords and would wear their master's livery as they travelled to proclaim his tournament. They became experts in armory as well as coats of arms.

They travelled on campaign as well, where they were granted safe passage by the armies of both sides. Part of their job was to keep a record of squires knighted before and after battle, of acts of chivalry and of deaths during battles. They also served as diplomats, carrying messages

from one army to the other. Another role was in the dramas of courtly love, when heralds were often used to carry messages between lovers.

HERALDIC DISPUTES

The 14th century saw the frequent appearance of heraldic treatises, usually written by heralds themselves. The heralds became involved in regulating coats of arms and their use. One knight could not simply use another's armorial bearings, or elements from its design, in his own coat of arms. By the 14th century, there were regulations in place in England to prevent a knight adopting a particular coat of arms unless it had royal approval or that of a high-ranking herald. In England, disputes were settled in the Court of Chivalry, founded in the 14th century.

▼ *A 15th-century manuscript illustrates some of the heraldic devices of the time.*

CHAPTER SIX

THE DECLINE OF THE KNIGHT

The Battle of Crécy in 1346 saw the first appearance on a battlefield of a new weapon that was severely to undermine the power of the mounted knight – the artillery gun. As the French advanced, their Genoese crossbowmen unleashed an assault on the English, who fought back with their longbowmen and a volley of fire from cannon. The Genoese fled, but the French continued their advance. Italian chronicler Giovanni Villani reported that at the battle's end 'the entire plain was strewn with men brought low by arrows and cannon balls'. Crécy was still a high point in the age of chivalry but the social, political and military changes that were to make chivalry outmoded can be traced back to this date.

Social and political conditions were becoming significantly different from those that had brought knighthood into being – the feudal system was eroding, and the nature of war was altering as kings needed armies for long-distance campaigns. Knights were becoming a minority in armies, and were generally fighting for a fee rather than as a feudal duty to their lord. The rise of the bowmen, the use of infantry and the appearance of artillery made knights less effective as a fighting force. At the same time, the ideal of an international chivalric brotherhood had been deflated as the Crusades petered out in disillusionment and failure. Knights were increasingly grouped in secular brotherhoods, devoted to the service of an earthly rather than heavenly sovereign. These changes played out over the following 250 years, with the result that by the 17th century knights had become something of an anachronism.

▲ *Cannon are depicted in a scene from a siege in 1400.*

◄ *The cannon at the Battle of Crécy marked a change in the character of warfare.*

THE CHANGING FACE OF WARFARE
THE RISE OF INFANTRY AND THE LONGBOW

Changes in military tactics and the evolving nature of warfare reduced the importance of knights riding into battle as cavalry. The increasing use of disciplined infantry lines, and the effectiveness of bowmen against a cavalry charge, increasingly meant that knights were no longer masters of the field of battle in their traditional role.

ARCHERS VERSUS KNIGHTS

It was once proudly declared by English historians that their country's famous victories over much larger French armies in the Hundred Years War were built on the heroic achievement of yeoman archers. However, this traditional view is now seen as rather outmoded and partisan. The more modern view, while arguing that the longbowmen were not decisive in battle, nevertheless accepts that they played a crucial role – the archers blunted the force

▼ *The Battle of Agincourt began with an exchange of arrows and crossbow bolts before the French cavalry made the first charge. The English archers then unleashed a storm of arrows, driving the French knights back into their own footsoldiers.*

of the charge made by the enemy knights, who were then turned back by the lines of infantry. These infantry lines played the decisive role. They included knights who had dismounted to fight on foot.

THE POWER OF THE LONGBOW

It is easy to see why the longbowmen played such an important part. The arrows unleashed by English bowmen in the army of King Edward III at Crécy in 1346,

▲ *Crossbowmen operate their powerful weapons during a siege of Wartburg Castle, Germany, in the early 14th century.*

or that of Henry V at Agincourt in 1415, could knock knights out of the saddle and rip into a horse's flank, sending the beast crashing to the ground and spilling the rider on to the mud. The archers used yew bows of 1.5–1.8m (5–6ft) in length, strung with hemp. Ordinary arrows were of aspen wood with a conventional tip, but the archers also used heavier ash-and-oak arrows capable of piercing a knight's armour – these were 83cm (33in) long with a very narrow 'bodkin' point. The archers sometimes used arrows with 5cm (2in)-wide barbed heads designed to dig into the side of the enemy horse.

The archers' extraordinary effectiveness in battle derived principally from their ability to fire as many as 15 arrows a minute, one every four seconds, to create a volley. They used a high trajectory so that the arrows rained down on the enemy from above in a deadly storm. They also drove sharp angled stakes into the ground, pointing at the enemy, and stood among them as they fired. As the remnants of the

▲ *In the armies of Europe, mounted and unmounted crossbowmen, often mixed with javeliners and archers, occupied a central position in battle formations.*

enemy cavalry charge came upon them, they withdrew backwards, still firing, and the enemy horses and their riders impaled themselves on the stakes.

THE DEVELOPMENT OF THE CROSSBOW

Bowmen in medieval armies used the crossbow as well as the longbow. The crossbow had a bigger range and better penetrative effect against armour than the longbow. The weapons came into widespread use in Europe as early as the 10th and 11th centuries when crossbows were frequently used in sieges by specialist mercenaries from Genoa (northern Italy) or Gascony (south-west France).

The first crossbows were made mainly of yew wood and horn, and fired a bolt, or 'quarrel', around 30cm (12in) long with a pointed steel head. They had a range of about 275m (900ft) but were difficult to load, and as the weapons were made more powerful they were usually fitted with a windlass to bend the bow. Crossbow bolts were very effective against chain mail – and, as discussed earlier, the desire to provide some protection against the bolt was

▶ *Duelling with hand-axes at tournaments gave knights the necessary practice in fighting on foot.*

one of the key incentives for those who sought to improve knights' armour. In the 15th century even more powerful steel crossbows were developed, with a range of up to 450m (1,500ft). They used a square-headed bolt that was strong enough to crack plate armour.

VULNERABLE TO CHANGE

Knights were not well equipped to cope with changes in military technology. As a class they were conservative – while knights dismounted to fight on foot with the infantry, no member of the chivalric class would have considered becoming an archer. Bows were the weapons of the lower classes: crossbows were initially the weapons of specialist Italian mercenaries, while the archers who won great victories for English armies were peasants. Moreover, the bow was considered to be

an unchivalric weapon because it encouraged fighting from a safe distance rather than in a face-to-face trial involving strength and prowess. Knights considered that using a bow was a sign of cowardice. The early 12th-century *chanson de geste* about the Burgundian chief Girart de Roussillon declares: 'May curses descend upon the first man who fought as an archer, for through fear he did not dare enter the fray.'

THE DECLINE OF KNIGHTHOOD

Military changes did not suddenly do away with knights in an instant. Both longbowmen and crossbowmen were a long-term problem for knights, dating back almost to the first years of chivalry. As early as 1139, Pope Innocent II had condemned 'the deadly art, which God hates, of crossbowmen and archers, must not be used against Christian knights on pain of anathema'; the effect of longbowmen was demonstrated in King Edward I of England's campaigns in Wales in the late 13th century, but knights continued to be an effective force long after that. The changes in military technology, the tactics of warfare, and the subsequent undermining of the role of knights, were slow and gradual – over centuries. In addition, these military evolutions are difficult to separate from the parallel social, political and cultural changes that were also contributing to the decline of the knight.

THE CANNON AND THE MUSKET

THE FIRST GUNS IN BATTLE

One key aspect of the military changes that undermined the importance of knights in battle was the introduction of the gun. Many of the early guns were difficult and dangerous to use, and they were often inaccurate, but they could be deadly even against full plate armour. Their introduction changed the balance of power on the battlefield, serving to weaken the strength of mounted knights and the use of cavalry as an offensive force.

THE ORIGINS OF GUNS

Gunpowder was probably invented in China, although some scholars argue that Arabs or even the peoples of ancient India were the first to develop the substance. One of the earliest guns was invented by Arabs in 1304: it was a tube of bamboo strengthened with iron, that fired an arrow using the explosive power of an early form of gunpowder called black powder. Gunpowder came to Europe in the mid-13th century – the English Franciscan philosopher Roger Bacon (c.1214–94) described its military uses – but guns of any sort were not widely used in battle until the 14th century.

▼ *John of Gaunt, Duke of Lancaster, used cannon during an assault on the town of Brest, France, in 1373.*

EARLY USE OF CANNON

Cannon were wheeled guns that fired iron balls or stones. The earliest reference to their manufacture is from 1326, when the city of Florence acquired two of the guns for defence. The first use of cannon in open battle was at Crécy in 1346.

There was a very wide range of heavy guns, with a wonderful variety of names including veuglaires, vasili, sclopi, pots-de-fer, crapaudines and serpentines. Very heavy cannon called bombards were developed in c.1380. Like many early guns they were inefficient and dangerous.

▲ *Firing produced a strong recoil, which was absorbed into the ground at the rear of the gun and through the wooden support.*

A later example of the bombard was Mons Meg, made for King James II of Scotland in 1449. It could fire shots weighing 180kg (396lb), and was one of the biggest types of bombard ever made.

Because heavy guns of this sort were so difficult to move about, they were mostly deployed in sieges, where they could have devastating effects on both stone and human flesh. They only came into serious use towards the close of the Hundred Years War (1337–1453). However, there are surprisingly few reports of knights being killed by cannon fire – one victim was Jacques de Lalaing, a knight from Wallonia, Belgium, who was killed in this way at the siege of Poucques in 1453 while serving the Duke of Burgundy in putting down a revolt by the people of Ghent. (De Lalaing's exploits were recorded by the celebrated Burgundian chronicler and herald Jean Le Fevre, a veteran of Agincourt, where he fought on the English side, and a member of the Order of the Golden Fleece.)

▲ *Gunners were vulnerable to attack while operating these early hand-held guns, which were very difficult to load, light and control.*

GUNS IN ISLAMIC ARMIES

The development of firearms and heavy artillery proceeded apace in the armies of Islam. The Moors in Spain used a form of cannon for defending the cities of Seville (1248) and Niebia (1262) under siege. Moorish artillery experts served in the armies of the kings of Spain in the mid-14th century. At the siege of Algeciras in 1342, Moorish defenders used cannon to great effect against the Christian besiegers. (The earls of Derby and Salisbury took part in this siege and may well have helped promote the cannon in England.)

The Ottoman Turks were on the receiving end of cannon fire when they were repelled by Byzantine guns during the siege of Constantinople in 1396. They had their revenge when they used 68 Hungarian cannon including 13 huge guns, each with a bore of more than 90cm (35in) and firing projectiles weighing 320kg (700lb), in their capture of Constantinople in 1453.

HAND-HELD GUNS

The first hand-held guns were developed in the 13th century. Called hand *gonnes,* or hand cannon, they were used in Islamic armies fighting the Mongols in *c.*1260 and appear to have been in use in Europe in 1281 when Italian *scopettieri* ('carriers of guns') were listed as fighting alongside crossbowmen. Early hand-operated guns of the 13th and 14th centuries looked like small cannon attached to wooden poles. The infantryman held the barrel under his arm and ignited the powder – hoping that the whole thing did not explode in his face. The early hand-guns were slow to load and difficult to aim, but if a gunner scored a direct hit he could kill a fully armoured knight outright.

More accurate hand-guns such as the arquebus, or hackbut, were developed in the 15th and 16th centuries. They used round balls as missiles, which could kill a knight in plate armour at short range, but at long range would only dent his armour. (New plate armour of this period was tested by firing an arquebus at its breastplate and the dent from the ball would be made into a feature of the suit by surrounding it with engraving.) The arquebus was replaced by the matchlock musket in the late 16th century. This gun was as much as 2m (7ft) long and fired 4.5kg (10lb) shot, but could not be used in wet weather. During the 17th century the musket became the main weapon used by infantrymen, replacing the pike.

THE RISE OF GUNS

Knights despised gunners as much as they did bowmen, and in the early days Church authorities denounced them as the work of the devil. In practical terms guns had disadvantages: they were slow to load, of limited accuracy, the larger ones were difficult to transport and manoeuvre and, most of all, in bad weather they often could not be fired at all. But their advantages were that their missiles were more effective than arrows against plate armour, the guns were relatively cheap to produce and use in large numbers, and they could

be fired by troops with little or no training – in stark contrast to the longbow, which was so difficult to use properly that the archers needed to be members of an elite force, trained from childhood and even given a special diet.

CANNON AND NEW DEFENCES

The use of cannon in battle and sieges led to the development of new types of fortifications that were better able to withstand bombardment with cannonballs. The traditional medieval ring-shaped or square fortifications with perpendicular stone walls proved to be very vulnerable to cannon. In the mid-1400s in Italy the trace italienne, or star-shaped fort, was developed: this was a low-lying fortification, made from brick and earth since these materials, unlike stone, would not shatter when hit by a cannonball. It was designed in a star shape to give defenders the opportunity to provide covering fire from several different angles.

The first trace italienne fortifications were designed by the Florentine architect Antonio di Pietro Averlino (1400–69), also known as Filarete, in his *Trattato di architettura* ('Treatise on Architecture') of 1465. That great Renaissance man Michelangelo then put the theory into practice when he designed the earthwork fortifications for Florence. The style soon became widely popular, and was found outside Italy from the 1530s onwards.

▼ *The earliest cannon had to be moved into position by hand; the first wheeled gun carriages were developed in the 1400s.*

PAID TO FIGHT

THE RISE OF PROFESSIONAL SOLDIERS

The knight's military role was also undermined by the use of professional soldiers in armies. Beginning in the late 13th century, rulers in Europe had to force knighthood on wealthy landowners whose birth and wealth made them eligible to become a knight. This was a startling change from the situation in the previous two centuries, when achieving a knighthood was the crowning glory of many a life.

In England in 1292, for example, those gentlemen with an annual income of £40 per year or more were required to accept knighthood and its obligations. A principal reason why this kind of law was necessary is that the cost of equipping oneself as a knight, always high, had risen to such a level that many were unwilling to meet it. The recently developed plate armour was made by Italian and German specialists and was extremely expensive. Heavier armour meant that stronger horses needed to be bred: these, too, were very expensive, and a knight needed to take several with him on campaign because the horse, as we have seen, was a favourite target for the archers and was often killed beneath its rider during battle.

THE USE OF MERCENARIES

There was already a substantial history of paid soldiers and of mercenaries serving in armies. Mercenaries were skilled professionals who hired themselves out to the highest payer – such as the Genoese crossbowmen who were working in this way as early as the 11th century. From the time of King Henry I of England (r. 1100–35) onwards, there were some paid soldiers in otherwise feudal armies. Kings would accept *scutage* (payment) in lieu of feudal military service, and then use the money to pay soldiers.

The oldest surviving military contract in England is from 1213: Lord Robert of Berkeley agreed to provide military service, in company of ten knights, to meet a debt to King John of 500 marks. King Philip IV of France (r. 1285–1314) had a considerable proportion of his army in paid service, including cavalry known as gendarmes (from the French: *gens d'armes,* meaning 'men at arms').

The Hundred Years War (1337–1453) saw many paid soldiers in service on both sides. They were generally infantry or bowmen rather than knights, although King Charles VII of France had 1,500 cavalry serving for fixed pay. In this period Swiss mercenary infantrymen won a wide reputation for their discipline and effectiveness fighting with halberds (long spears with axe-like heads), with which they were able to haul a knight down from his horse. These men were available for hire, and their wearing of uniforms and marching to military music were widely influential. Under the influence of the Swiss, the first state infantry regiments were formed in France in the 1450s. This was part of a general movement in the 15th century towards the establishment of professional standing armies.

CONDOTTIERI

The same period saw the heyday of Italian mercenary bands of knights hired by competing Italian city-states. The leaders of these mercenary bands were called *condottieri,* from the Italian *condotta* for the 'contract' by which they tied themselves

▼ *Condottiere Guidoriccio da Fogliano was commander of the mercenary army of Siena, Italy in 1328, and he is commemorated in the famous fresco believed to be by Simone Martini.*

SIR JOHN HAWKWOOD

Leading *condottiere* Sir John Hawkwood came from humble origins as the son of a tanner in Essex, England. He achieved fame fighting in the army of King Edward III of England during the Hundred Years War, and was reputedly knighted for his battlefield prowess by the king or the Black Prince. In 1363, during a break in English–French

hostilities, he entered the White Company of Italian *condottieri* in the service of Pisa and was elected their captain within a year. He used his own force of longbowmen, and equipped his knights with lighter armour that made his troops more mobile. In *condottieri* fashion, by 1369 he was fighting for a new paymaster, Perugia, against papal troops and within a few years was fighting for the pope against Florence. He became immensely wealthy, with estates near Florence. Chivalry was a foreign concept to him: he would threaten his employers with desertion in order to get more money out of them. He died in Florence in 1394.

◄ *Sir John Hawkwood was known as 'Giovanni Acuto' in Italy. He married Donnina, illegitimate daughter of his then paymaster the Duke of Milan, in 1377.*

to a particular city or nobleman. The bands consisted principally of armoured knights fighting with traditional medieval weapons. The *condottieri* were famous for their ruthlessness and lack of chivalry: they would negotiate hard, driving their fee as high as they could, and were not above switching sides (even in the middle of a battle) if offered more money.

The first of these mercenary bands were non-Italians. The knights of the Catalan Company formed in 1303 had originally been in the service of King Peter III of Aragon, the Grand Company of *c.*1350 principally contained Hungarians and Germans. The English knight Sir John Hawkwood (see box) led the White Company in the wars of northern Italy for much of the second half of the 14th century.

▶ *Erasmo of Narni was a leading Italian mercenary knight in the late 14th century. His fame was such that the armour in which he fought was preserved for posterity, and Donatello immortalized him in stone.*

In the 15th century the *condottieri* were mostly made up of Italians, and were often noblemen fallen on hard times. Knights in these bands could make a great deal of money in a short period. Towards the close of the century, the *condottieri* bands were mostly overwhelmed by the heavy

artillery of the army of King Charles VIII of France, who invaded northern Italy to enforce his rather threadbare claim to the kingdom of Naples.

Probably the most famous *condottiere* was Erasmo di Narni, better known by his nickname Gattamelata ('Honeyed Cat'). He served Florence, Venice and the papacy and eventually became dictator of Padua in 1457. His renown was such that an equestrian statue of him by Donatello was erected in 1445–50, the first such statue since the days of the Roman Empire.

Another celebrated *condottiere* of the 16th century was Giovanni de' Medici (known as Giovanni delle Bande Nere – 'Giovanni of the Black Bands') who led a company of highly skilled Italian mercenaries during the Italian Wars. He initially fought for Pope Leo X in 1516–21 before switching sides in 1522 and joining the forces of Francis I of France. He then briefly went into the service of the Holy Roman Emperor, Charles V, before returning to French service. Giovanni was fighting in the army of Francis I when he was severely wounded at the Battle of Pavia in 1525. He died in 1526 after injuries sustained while fighting in the League of Cognac war. His name probably came from the black bands of mourning on his banner after the death of Pope Leo X in 1521.

THE END OF AN ERA
THE LAST DAYS OF CHIVALRY

▲ King from the age of 10, Richard II of England became known for arrogance and arbitrary government that encouraged plotting and factions at court and undermined the workings of chivalry.

By the 15th and 16th centuries both the feudal system and the chivalric tradition had undergone profound changes. The age of chivalry was coming to an end.

DECLINE OF FEUDALISM

The rise of towns in the late Middle Ages had undermined the relationship between a feudal lord and his bonded vassals, replacing it with the one between the king and his subjects or between an elected representative body and a citizen. Because of the increasing importance of merchants, and the trade that made them rich, money was becoming more important than land.

Military changes, as we have seen, played their part in a decline of feudalism. The mounted warrior lost status on the battlefield. The supreme symbol of feudal power, the castle, lost its image of impregnability with the advent of more and more effective siege weaponry and guns. Military architects began to build low-lying fortifications from earth and brick such as the trace italienne in place of traditional defences.

CHIVALRIC SHIFT

At the same time there were changes in the philosophical, religious and cultural tradition of chivalry, which had grown up around knighthood and come to sustain it. Despite the erosion of the feudal system, knighthood retained its romance, but it began to function in a different context.

The rise of national feeling had profound effects. The religious brotherhoods of chivalry, in which knights' primary duty was religious, through swearing loyalty to Christ and the brotherhood, were replaced by secular brotherhoods of chivalry such as England's Order of the Garter or the Order of the Star in France, in which knights swore loyalty to their king. The traditional chivalric ideal of an international elite of knights, all equal in their brotherhood, was replaced by bodies of knights tied to the service of their sovereign, conscious of national difference. Increasingly, distinctions of rank were made among knights, who once had been members of an equal brotherhood in which a humble warrior could be knighted on the battlefield for his prowess and become the equal of a prince.

Another contributing change was religious. The rise of Protestantism was associated with patriotism and national feeling and contributed to the undermining of the ideal of the international Christian brotherhood of knights. The humanistic philosophy of the Renaissance ran counter to the religious ardour that had sustained chivalry and driven knights to the Holy Land in the service of Christ.

PAGEANTS

Tournaments had once fulfilled a necessary role as martial training grounds, and provided an arena in which a man of relatively humble birth such as William

▼ Baldassare Castiglione (1478–1529), author of The Courtier, *ushered in a new concern with courtly etiquette among the nobility. When in Rome, he befriended the artist Raphael, who painted this portrait.*

Marshal could win sufficient honour to raise himself to the level of the upper nobility and of royalty. In the transformed world of the 15th and 16th centuries, tournaments were lavish affairs dominated by demonstrations of etiquette as much as prowess. Fighting became less important.

In the 13th and 14th centuries, lesser noblemen held their own tournaments, but the extravagant events of the next two centuries emphasized the pre-eminence of a prince or his near equivalents among the nobility. Tournaments increasingly became pageants, laid on by royal patrons, in order to demonstrate their own magnificence before their leading subjects. Chivalry stopped being a way of life and became an entertainment.

During this period, the chivalric romance that had embodied and sustained the philosophy of chivalry began to fade as a living literary form. Authors under the growing influence of Renaissance ideas turned to classical models. Tournaments abandoned the model of King Arthur and his knights and based their pageants on the warriors of the classical world.

COURTESY AND THE GENTLEMAN

The handbooks on chivalry that had once been so popular gave way to handbooks on courtesy. These books taught not how to be a knight but how to be a gentleman. An early example was *Il Cortegiano* (*The*

Courtier), written between 1513 and 1518 by the Italian courtier and diplomat Baldassare Castiglione. Presented in the form of discussions by courtiers at the Court of Urbino in 1507, the book considers how to act gracefully, with seeming effortlessness; the modesty and qualities that should mark a lady at court; how a courtier should avoid flattery in dealings with his prince; and what forms humour and honourable love should take.

◄ *Edward III confers the Order of the Garter on Edward the Black Prince. The creation of secular bodies of knights was at odds with the spirit of devotion that inspired the members of religious brotherhoods such as the Knights Templar and Hospitaller.*

The idealism of chivalric literature was notably absent in *The Courtier* and similar books on courtesy, which placed more emphasis on presentation, appearance and reputation than on virtues such as humility and bravery, so important in chivalry. In addition, the passion of courtly love was banished; a courtier was expected to show his prince the adoration and committed service that a knight showed his lady.

The gentleman replaced the knight as an ideal. He was a figure of society rather than a warrior. The key to being a gentleman was 'gentle birth': usually it was sufficient to show this status going back for three generations. The knight was a mounted warrior in origin with public status, but the gentleman had no such necessary function. By the end of the 16th century, the word 'knight' had become a title, and indication of social rank.

▼ *Flemish-born artist Marcus Gheeraerts the Elder engraved the procession of the Knights of the Garter in 1576, capturing the spirit of exclusiveness and refinement that was beginning to inform the brotherhood.*

THE ENDURING ROMANCE OF KNIGHTHOOD
REVIVALS OF CHIVALRY

Knighthood retained its romance throughout the long erosion of the feudal system and the decline of chivalric life. In the 16th and 17th centuries, and even later, princes and noblemen looked back with great enthusiasm on the glories of the age of chivalry. Occasionally, even into the 19th century, wealthy lords attempted to revive tournaments and other displays of knighthood.

TUDOR TOURNAMENTS
In England the monarchs of the late Tudor era were already looking back on the golden age of chivalry. Knighthood held a powerful appeal for them – particularly for King Henry VIII, who was a keen patron of and participant in tournaments. Henry designed some of his own armour for competing in tournaments and had an armoury established at Greenwich, near

▼ At the Field of the Cloth of Gold in 1520, kings Francis I and Henry VIII erected grand temporary buildings and tournament lists that made the area resemble a city.

London. He established tiltyards for holding tournaments at Greenwich, adjacent to Whitehall Palace (in Westminster) and at Hampton Court Palace (now part of south-west London).

Henry was matched in his devotion to tournaments by King Francis I of France, and their diplomatic meeting near Calais on 7–24 June 1520 was celebrated with an extraordinarily lavish show of the arts of chivalry. In line with the 15th-century *pas d'armes* ('passage of arms') that the kings were emulating, the event was extravagantly stage-managed.

The two kings and their retinues, numbering 5,000, camped in an array of tents and pavilions decorated with cloth of gold (a fabric made with gold thread and silk) – and for this reason the event became popularly known as the Field of the Cloth of Gold. Henry's camp took the form of a temporary palace – mainly built of canvas and painted cloth over timber frames – measuring 10,000sq m (108,000sq ft). Outside Henry's tent was a gilded fountain spouting claret, spiced wine and water.

Each king had a company of seven knights, supplemented by those who had arrived in response to proclamation of the event and who chose to fight on one side or the other. The kings jousted one against the other, and against the opposing team's knights. Upwards of 300 spears were broken, and one French knight was killed. After the jousting there was a form of tournament, but the knights fought in pairs rather than in an old-fashioned mêlée. There were also contests in archery and the two kings reputedly wrestled for a few throws. The kings and the knights dressed in great splendour in an attempt to revive the glories of the age of chivalry.

ACCESSION DAY TILTS
Henry's daughter, Elizabeth, continued the chivalric revival. On 17 November each year from 1570 until 1590 she celebrated the anniversary of her accession to the throne in 1558 with an 'Accession Day Tilt' at Whitehall Palace. The events were part of a deliberate official mythologizing of Elizabeth as a reigning goddess, and

▲ *Elizabeth I of England shared her father's enthusiasm for the age of chivalry and carried on his revival of tournament events.*

aimed also to replace some of the colour and popular entertainment of Catholic feast days, held no more under the Protestant Elizabeth. Her champion, Henry Lee, was one of her favourites, and he rode in her name in the tiltyard established by Henry VIII in the royal palace at Whitehall while the queen and her ladies, situated in a raised palace window, looked down on the chivalric exploits beneath them like ladies at one of the medieval tournaments.

Even in the beginning of the Stuart era in the early 17th century, the enthusiasm for the age of chivalry endured, and King James I's son Henry, Prince of Wales, was a keen jouster. But he died aged just 18 of typhoid fever in 1612. Thereafter, courtly interest in the chivalric tradition in England was focused on the court masques of Ben Jonson and Inigo Jones.

THE CARROUSEL

Events fashioned like tournaments continued to be held in continental Europe. The jousting and tourneying shrank to near disappearing point, while centre stage was given to displays of horsemanship in events called 'carrousels'. The knights in these extravaganzas often wore imitation

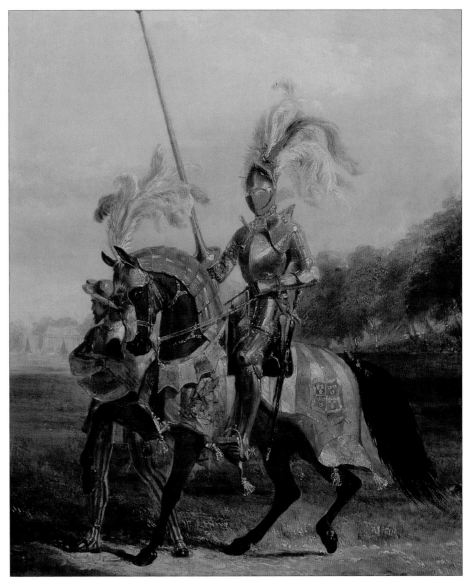

armour. The purpose was to make a show of the magnificence of the sponsor of the event. In time, these gave way to military parades, which fulfilled the same purpose.

INTO THE VICTORIAN ERA

Grand revivals of chivalric tournaments occurred as late as 1839, when the 13th Earl of Eglington held a tournament with jousting at Eglington Castle in Ayrshire. A great crowd of noble guests, enthused by the 19th-century revival of interest in chivalry and medieval life, wore medieval costumes and watched as knights paid homage to Lady Georgiana Sheridan, the Duke of Somerset's wife, in her guise as the event's 'Queen of Beauty'. However, the event was effectively rained off by a Scottish storm that made a mud bath of

▲ *Archibald Montgomerie, 13th Earl of Eglington, had an authentic-looking suit of armour made for his tournament of 1839.*

the lists. Two years in the planning, the event cost no less than £40,000 – the knightly way of life never did come cheap.

THE IDEAL KNIGHT

Right through to the 21st century, the knight has kept much of his lustre as a composite of nobleman and warrior, an idealized expression of personal honour, respectful devotion and religious fervour. His continued appeal is due as much to the knight's role in chivalric literature, with its enduringly popular narratives and affecting elegiac tone, as it is to his historical achievements.

INDEX

▲ *A medieval joust.*

▼ *King Arthur's homecoming.*

▲ *Lancelot and Guinevere.*

▼ *A castle and its vassals.*

▲ *Beaumaris Castle.*

▼ *Medieval heraldic devices.*

▲ A knight at prayer.

▼ The Battle of Crécy.

This edition is published by Hermes House,
an imprint of Anness Publishing Ltd,
Hermes House, 88–89 Blackfriars Road,
London SE1 8HA
tel. 020 7401 2077; fax 020 7633 9499

www.hermeshouse.com; www.annesspublishing.com

If you like the images in this book and would like to investigate using them for publishing, promotions or advertising, please visit our website www.practicalpictures.com for more information.

Publisher: Joanna Lorenz
Editorial Director: Helen Sudell, Executive Editor: Joanne Rippin
Illustrations: Simon Smith
Designer: Nigel Partridge
Production Controller: Christine Ni

ETHICAL TRADING POLICY: At Anness Publishing we believe that business should be conducted in an ethical and ecologically sustainable way, with respect for the environment and a proper regard to the replacement of the natural resources we employ.
As a publisher, we use a lot of wood pulp in high-quality paper for printing, and that wood commonly comes from spruce trees. We are therefore currently growing more than 750,000 trees in three Scottish forest plantations: Berrymoss (130 hectares/320 acres), West Touxhill (125 hectares/305 acres) and Deveron Forest (75 hectares/185 acres). The forests we manage contain more than 3.5 times the number of trees employed each year in making paper for the books we manufacture. Because of this ongoing ecological investment programme, you, as our customer, can have the pleasure and reassurance of knowing that a tree is being cultivated on your behalf to naturally replace the materials used to make the book you are holding.
Our forestry programme is run in accordance with the UK Woodland Assurance Scheme (UKWAS) and will be certified by the internationally recognized Forest Stewardship Council (FSC). The FSC is a non-government organization dedicated to promoting responsible management of the world's forests. Certification ensures forests are managed in an environmentally sustainable and socially responsible way. For further information about this scheme, go to www.annesspublishing.com/trees

PUBLISHER'S NOTE: Although the advice and information in this book are believed to be accurate and true at the time of going to press, neither the authors nor the publisher can accept any legal responsibility or liability for any errors or omissions that may have been made.

ACKNOWLEDGEMENTS: The publishers wish to thank the following agencies for the use of their images. Art Archive: pp1, 3, 5 & 14, 7t, 11b, 13, 14, 16t, 16b, 17t, 17b. 18t, 18b, 19t, 19b, 20, 21, 21b, 22, 23l, 23r, 24t, 24b, 25b, 26, 30, 31t, 31b, 32t, 34, 36, 37bl, 37br, 38t, 41tl, 42, 43t, 45b, 52t, 59tl, 59tr, 60, 62b, 64, 71t, 73t, 75b, 80, 83t, 86, 88t, 88b, 89t, 89b, 91, 92, 93b, 93t, 95, 96b, 98b, 99, 100t, 101t, 108t, 108b, 109t, 110t, 110b, 113, 114t, 114b, 115t, 115b, 116t, 116t, 117b, 119t, 120t, 124.
AKG: pp2, 5, 7b, 10b, 15, 17, 25, 27, 28b, 32b, 33t, 33b, 37t, 38b, 39t, 39b, 41tr, 41b, 45t, 53t, 56, 59b, 51t, 65, 67, 71b, 73b, 77t, 77b, 78, 79, 87, 90, 96t, 98t, 100, 101b, 106t, 117t, 120b.
Bridgeman Art Library: pp5, 6, 8t, 8b, 9t, 9b, 10t, 11t, 12, 28bl, 28t, 29, 40b, 40t, 43b, 44, 46b. 47b, 48, 49t, 58, 52b, 54t, 55t, 57tl, 57tr & 51, 57b, 61b, 62t, 63, 66, 72, 74t, 74t, 74b, 75t, 78b, 81bl, 82b, 82t, 84t, 84b, 85b, 94, 97t, 102b, 103t, 104, 105t, 105b, 109b, 111t, 111b, 112, 118t, 119b, 121t, 121b, 122, 123tr, 123tl, 128.
istock images: pp29, 35, 48t, 54, 72, 76, 81, 102, 103.